UNLIMITING
GOD

RICHARD BLACKABY

MULTNOMAH
BOOKS

UNLIMITING GOD
PUBLISHED BY MULTNOMAH BOOKS
12265 Oracle Boulevard, Suite 200
Colorado Springs, Colorado 80921
A division of Random House Inc.

All Scripture quotations are taken from the New King James Version®. Copyright ©
1982 by Thomas Nelson Inc. Used by permission. All rights reserved.

Italics in Scripture quotations indicate the author's added emphasis.

ISBN 978-1-59052-941-6

Copyright © 2008 by Richard Blackaby

Library of Congress Cataloging-in-Publication Data
Blackaby, Richard, 1961–
    Unlimiting God: increasing your capacity to experience the divine / Richard
Blackaby.—1st ed.
        p. cm.
    Includes bibliographical references.
    ISBN 978-1-59052-941-6
    1. Spiritual life—Christianity. 2. God (Christianity)—Knowableness. I. Title.
    BV4501.3.B534 2007
    248.4—dc22
                                        2007028726

Printed in the United States of America

2008—First Edition

10 9 8 7 6 5 4 3 2 1

Special Sales
Most WaterBrook Multnomah books are available in special quantity discounts when
purchased in bulk by corporations, organizations, and special interest groups. Custom
imprinting or excerpting can also be done to fit special needs. For information, please
e-mail SpecialMarkets@WaterBrookPress.com or call 1-800-603-7051.

To my father, Henry Blackaby,
the greatest man of God I have ever known.

CONTENTS

THE PROBLEM IS NEVER WITH GOD

For the past several years, our family has spent the last weekend in August at my brother-in-law Jim's home in Taber, Alberta, Canada. Taber is famous for its bumper crop of succulent corn. Every year the small town hosts Cornfest to celebrate the harvest. The festivities include a carnival, outdoor concerts, a craft fair, and fireworks, plus 5k and 10k runs.

Five years ago my daughter Carrie decided she wanted to join the rest of the family on the run. Carrie is a marvelous ice skater, but she'd never participated in a formal footrace before. I decided the fatherly thing to do was to let her run with me. In my younger days, my keen competitive instincts would have steered me clear of any impediment that might hinder my chances at a medal. But after undergoing decades of God's teaching me life's true priorities, having gained much wisdom in my middle age, and having put on fifty pounds since my university days, I decided to forgo any chance of finishing near the top. I offered to run with my little daughter.

Carrie, knowing her dad's competitive nature, demanded assurance that I wouldn't abandon her in the heat of the race. I promised her I was running only for enjoyment and it would be great fun to accompany her—regardless of where we placed. In fact, I said, anytime she wanted to stop running and start walking to catch her breath, I'd happily comply.

The starting gun fired. My wife and two sons were among the "keeners" at the front of the pack, and they quickly disappeared from sight around the first bend.

As my daughter and I loped along at an easy pace on that beautiful morning, I joked with her and encouraged her.

After only two blocks, Carrie wanted to slow to a walk. It seemed a little early for our first rest break, but I told her that was fine by me. Dozens of young people whizzed past us as we leisurely walked along enjoying the morning air.

After a few minutes I asked Carrie if she was ready to try running again. She was. But after only a few more blocks, she asked to walk again. No problem. Young adults were streaming by. Then middle-aged people began passing us. Some older women were overtaking us at a brisk walk.

> *That was too much. "I will NOT lose to THEM!" I wheezed.*

I exhorted my weary daughter to dig a little deeper so we could push forward. We ran, but soon she was complaining that her side hurt. I reluctantly agreed to walk again. In this pattern, our "race" continued.

Then it happened. I heard them coming. I was surprised anyone was still behind us, but sure enough, a middle-aged woman pushing her elderly mother *in a wheelchair* serenely glided past, leaving us to eat their dust.

That was too much. "I will NOT lose to THEM!" I wheezed. "I've got my limits!"

We staggered off at a trot. I could just make out the finish line on the horizon. My legs were aching. My breath was coming in short, painful gasps. But we were slowly gaining on the wheelchair.

Then Carrie, too, noticed the crowds cheering and waving at the finish line in the distance. Suddenly she underwent a metamorphosis. The hesitant little girl I'd been tenderly coaxing throughout the race immediately found her second wind. She accelerated rapidly. The lights had come on. She was possessed.

Carrie torpedoed past the wheelchair, her eye on the prize.

I tried to keep up, but there were only fumes left in my tank. I made a heroic last effort, barely edging out the octogenarian and her daughter before crossing the tape.

Carrie waited for me at the finish line with a water bottle and a handful of fruit. She wasn't even winded.

Later that day, we were met with a huge surprise. At the awards ceremony, Carrie received a beautiful first-place medal for her age category. (They handed out oxygen masks for mine.) I'm so glad Carrie grew dissatisfied with her performance, even though she had no idea a prize was waiting for her just around the corner.

Carrie has since won another medal, and as I write this, she's training for a 10k race coming up soon.

What's my point? My daughter always had the ability to be a medal-winning runner, but she'd set the limit for herself far below her capacity. She might have been satisfied to remain there too, had I not finally urged her to push on to another level.

The Bible describes the Christian life as a race (1 Corinthians 9:24–27; Philippians 3:12–14; 2 Timothy 4:7). This Christian race is one in which every participant has an equal opportunity to be spectacularly successful. It all depends on how much the person wants to succeed.

The apostle Paul claimed he ran life's race to win the prize (1 Corinthians 9:24). Unfortunately, many Christians set their sights far too low. They're satisfied to plod along in dreary, unrewarding spirituality, unwilling to pay the price for greater spiritual accomplishments. They may be comfortable, but they're not experiencing nearly as much as they could. They've inadvertently chosen to limit their experience of God.

Here's another picture. God invites His people to a richer experience: "Call to Me, and I will answer you, and show you great and mighty things, which you do not know" (Jeremiah 33:3). Almighty, infinite, all-knowing God welcomes people to come to Him and to allow Him to reveal things from His heart and mind that would amaze them. Yet when was the last time you learned something brand-new from God that was "great and mighty"? Many Christians today receive this enormous invitation, and yet we rarely experience a fresh, dynamic encounter with God. It's not that the Lord isn't willing to reveal more exciting truths to us; we limit our own capacity to receive more from Him.

The problem is never with God. The obstacle is us. We're far too easily satisfied. We limit God in our lives.

God "is able to do exceedingly abundantly above all that we ask or think, according to the power that works in us" (Ephesians 3:20). Have you seen Him do things in and through your life that absolutely amaze you in their magnitude? If you haven't, why is that? After all, the Bible says God wants you to experience this.

Again, the impediment is not God. The problem lies with us. We've become too easily satisfied with spiritual mediocrity. Some of us have become so used to a powerless life that we've come to think of it as normal for the Christian. It is not. God has more for us to experience and to do than we could imagine. We limit God's activity by our own choices.

This book is for those whose spiritual lives suffer from self-imposed limits. Does that describe you? Have you grown complacent in your walk with God? Do you assume you've already reached the pinnacle of what you're going to experience in your Christian life? Wouldn't you rather grow stronger in your faith, enjoy new victories, and reach higher levels in your walk with God?

Whatever unnecessary limits you've accepted in your spiritual life, my prayer is that you'll determine to break through the barriers that keep you from reaching an entirely new level in your relationship with God. It's time to unlimit God in our lives and to invite Him to do what He longs to do in and through

> *This book is for those whose spiritual lives suffer from self-imposed limits.*

us—knowing that He's prepared to respond to whatever it is we seek from Him.

I've had the tremendous privilege of traveling around the world and seeing God's kingdom expanding on six continents. I've met incredible Christians and been in dynamic churches that are experiencing God working through them in amazing ways. But I've also sensed the spiritual lostness among teeming multitudes in Asia, in massive townships in Africa, in isolated villages on the Amazon, and among affluent, spiritually indifferent crowds of businesspeople in downtown districts of the world's major cities. Clearly, despite all the modern church is doing to extend God's kingdom, it's not enough. We're losing ground. The number of unbelievers worldwide is growing faster than the numbers of believers.

I've worshiped with fellow Christians from around the world as we praised God for His mighty power. Yet God's power seems to be in short supply in many churches today. Countless congregations are divided, many others have reached a plateau or begun a steady decline—yet they sing every Sunday of God's awesome strength.

Clearly the status quo of modern Christianity is inadequate. More of the same won't bring us any closer to God's rule on earth. As Christians today we must reach an entirely new plane in our walk with God. Churches must believe and serve their Lord at a higher level than they've experienced so far. There's too much at stake for Christians and churches to keep doing business as usual.

God is looking for people who are willing to pay the price to obtain a qualitatively different walk with Him. Will you be one of those people? Are you prepared to unlimit God in your life so you can experience Him the way He has always wanted you to?

ONE

EXCEEDING THE LIMITS

People have their limits. Some choose to ignore them.

On May 4, 2006, I sat in the East Room of the White House next to my wife, Lisa. Gathered in that ornate room were my four siblings and their spouses, along with my parents, various White House officials and government leaders, and President George W. Bush. My father, honorary chairman of the National Day of Prayer, stood on the small dais at the center of the room and offered a prayer for the nation.

As he concluded and prepared to descend the platform, President Bush began to ascend the steps to the podium. Before the distinguished group of dignitaries, he smiled warmly and shook my father's hand. I captured a picture of that moment, and I have it framed in my office. It isn't often someone watches his father shake hands and exchange greetings with the president of the United States. That same day, President Bush informed my father that every morning he reads *Experiencing God Day by Day*, a devotional book my father and I wrote.

As I was enjoying that special occasion, I had a bizarre thought. It occurred to me that my father is one of the most ordinary people I know. I mused, *What if the White House discovers that this man they're treating with such respect is actually, in fact, an ordinary person? Would Secret Service agents roughly show him (and his ordinary family) to the door?*

OUT OF THE ORDINARY

Let me hasten to say my dad is the godliest man I know. I've had the privilege of meeting several famous Christian leaders whom I greatly admire, but my father is hands down the greatest man of God I've known. All the same, he's a very ordinary person.

Henry Thomas Blackaby was born in Williams Lake, British Columbia, Canada. (He likes to add, "Not in the lake, but in the town.") His father and my grandfather, Gerald Richard Blackaby, was the branch manager of the Bank of Montreal and a fascinating man. He had strong convictions and didn't worry if they made him unpopular. At the outset of World War I, the bank's executive management feared the bank would lose its best staff to the military. So they warned employees that those who left the bank to enlist would not have their positions held for them during the war. My grandfather immediately enlisted in the army anyway. He fought in many of the major battles and was wounded in a mustard-gas attack. When he returned to work at war's end, he was placed in the managerial doghouse and consigned to the worst postings.

Soon after my father's birth, my grandfather was transferred to Prince Rupert, a town located on Canada's west coast, close to the Alaska border. It was even more isolated from civilization than Williams Lake. The Prince Rupert area came as close as anything to Canada's Wild West. It was surrounded by mines from which miners descended on the town every weekend seeking fun (and/or trouble). It was a port city as well as a railroad hub, so sailors and railway workers looking for mischief populated the streets. There were also several First Nations tribes in that area that regularly experienced conflict with the townspeople. When all those forces convened in that isolated place, trouble was inevitable.

That was where my father grew up. It wasn't necessarily a nursery for greatness.

When the family first arrived in Prince Rupert, my granddad immediately began looking for a church home. Not finding one that he believed was true to the Scriptures, he promptly started his own. With his own funds he rented a dance hall, and each Sunday morning, on the sidewalk outside the hall, he put a small clapboard sign he'd constructed that read, "Christ: Crucified, Crowned, Coming."

For eight months the only congregants were my grandparents, my father, and his two brothers. Their first visitor was a man whose life had been ravaged by alcohol. He was intending to commit suicide when he stumbled across this tiny church and was gloriously converted.

In this humble church environment, my father learned about God and began his Christian walk. Ultimately that meager congregation grew to become the largest evangelical church in the area.

Two years ago, I took my son Mike with me when I traveled to the Middle East to speak in a church. At the close of my sermon, a couple eagerly approached

It wasn't necessarily a nursery for greatness.

me and introduced themselves. They told us, "We became Christians in the church your grandfather started in Prince Rupert." Amazing. Seventy years after my grandfather began that church, his grandson and great-grandson were meeting people in the Middle East who were still grateful for his faithfulness.

How did this upbringing affect my father? He certainly learned to hold fast to his convictions. He also grew to be an extremely shy young man. In fact, he was so soft-spoken that when he preached his first sermon, people sitting more than three rows from the front could barely hear a word he said. Today my father is a powerful preacher, but I wouldn't describe him as an unusually gifted orator. Nor is he an outstanding administrator. And no one has ever accused him of being cutting edge in his ministry techniques.

As I said, he's extremely ordinary.

Yet here he was, an introverted Canadian from an isolated northern town, in the White House shaking hands with the president. That same month he was invited to speak to a gathering of forty ambassadors at the United Nations. He regularly counsels and mentors 165 Christian CEOs of Fortune 500 companies. He has preached in 112 countries and continues to be a popular speaker and writer. His book *Experiencing God: Knowing and Doing His Will* has been translated into more than seventy languages and has sold millions of copies.

One cannot escape the obvious conclusion: here's a man who allowed God to overcome his natural limitations and to make him a person of great spiritual influence.

People Who Rose Above Their Limitations

I love to read biographies. It fascinates me to study the lives of people who had a dramatic impact on the world for Christ. Almost without exception, they were ordinary men and women whom God enabled to overcome their limiting factors so they could achieve great things for His kingdom.

One of my favorite historical characters is Dwight L. Moody. He was an uneducated layman. In fact, his grammar was so poor that his fellow church members asked him to refrain from speaking at church meetings because it was so painful to listen to him. When he sought admission into church membership, he failed a simple test measuring rudimentary Bible knowledge. He volunteered to teach Sunday school, but his church wouldn't trust him with an existing class. He had to begin a new one and enlist his own students. Despite his numerous and obvious limitations, he became the greatest evangelist of his day, encouraging thousands of people to serve in Christian ministry and missions.

Charles Spurgeon had no formal ministerial training, yet he became such a popular preacher in London that people had to obtain a ticket to gain access to his Sunday services.

Fanny Crosby went blind as a baby as the result of a dangerous medical treatment from someone impersonating a doctor. Her father died soon after. Yet Crosby would eventually write over nine thousand hymns, many of them cherished favorites. She became personally acquainted with most of the American presidents who served during her lifetime.

Duncan Campbell, a Presbyterian pastor in Scotland, spent seventeen years in mundane parish ministry. One day he grew so dissatisfied with the meager fruit of his labors he cried out for God's anointing on his life. Henceforth Campbell became God's mighty catalyst for revival wherever he went.

> *They were ordinary men and women whom God enabled to overcome their limiting factors.*

Jonathan Goforth was a Canadian Presbyterian missionary to China. He wrote this about his early ministry: "I began to experience a growing dissatisfaction with the results of my work. In the early pioneer years I had buoyed myself with the assurance that a seed time must always precede a harvest, and had, therefore, been content to persist in the apparently futile struggle. But now thirteen years had passed, and the harvest seemed, if anything, farther away than ever."[1] It was only after Goforth became totally discontented with the results of his life and ministry that God did a powerful transforming work in him. God then used him mightily during the Shantung Revival, through which large numbers of Chinese people experienced salvation and revival.

The first time young Billy Graham preached, he was so intimidated that he nervously delivered his entire repertoire of four sermons in eight minutes. Despite this unspectacular beginning, he surrendered his life entirely to his Lord's service and went on to preach to more people than anyone else in history.

IN OUR DAY AS WELL

The same dramatic breakthroughs are happening today. God continues to enable ordinary believers to overcome their limiting factors. It's been my privilege to meet many of these dynamic Christians all around the world, and their stories are as diverse as they are amazing.

There's the blind pastor I met in Africa who was invited by a woman to start a church in her community. The man and his wife responded, and despite his physical limitations, that church grew and flourished. The Sunday I was there, four overcrowded services held more than fifteen hundred people.

What sets them apart?

A woman in the United States has a heart for orphans in Asia, and God has used her to develop an extensive ministry to them.

A retired businessman was reluctant to squander his leisure years, so he started two companies for the purpose of investing the profits into the kingdom of God. Both ventures have prospered.

I know an entrepreneur in Manila who had a passion for reaching businesspeople in the Philippines. He left his lucrative career and is now the pastor of one of the largest churches in Manila.

A former alcoholic in Brazil is now a church planter. God is leading him to start churches along a stretch of the Amazon River with almost ninety villages. When he took me with him to visit the site of his latest church plant, he shared that he'd begun works in fifty-seven of those villages and was aggressively working to reach the rest.

A young executive of a major financial-services corporation leads his company to give half its profits to Christian ministries.

A group of businessmen felt burdened for the men of their city, so they began an interdenominational men's ministry that is impacting thousands of men today.

A doctor in Malaysia left his medical practice to minister to people's souls and is now the pastor of one of the most dynamic churches in that country.

These are people I've met in the last two years. They're all ordinary men and women who've asked God to overcome the limits in their lives so they can make an impact for His kingdom. Most aren't endued with extraordinary giftedness. In fact, they will all testify to some extreme limitations.

So what sets them apart?

- They have a profound personal intimacy with God.
- They're experiencing God's power in their lives in biblical proportions.
- God is using them to accomplish far more for His kingdom than they dreamed was possible.
- They're experiencing the joy of the Lord to an unusual degree.

COMPELLING QUESTIONS

I've lived my entire life around Christians who had a profound walk with God. God has also worked mightily through many of my family members and close friends. This wonderful heritage has led me to ask several compelling questions:

- If God is truly all powerful, why doesn't He manifest His awesome strength more often through more of His people?
- With millions of Christians around the world worshiping and praying each week, why isn't God's power evident in more congregations? Furthermore, why are so many churches struggling and dying?
- If God wants to reach the millions of people around the world who do not know Him, why doesn't He perform greater miracles through Christians who are serving Him?
- Why do so many Christians find it boring to spend time with God in prayer, Bible study, and worship?
- Since God is limitless, why do so many Christians know Him only on a surface level?
- God can do anything—so why are so many Christians defeated and discouraged?
- Considering God's numerous promises, why are there so many joyless Christians?

I know I'm not the only one who wonders these things. I read the Bible and see how wondrous God is. I list His incredible promises. Yet I encounter hundreds of Christians whose lives are one prolonged struggle.

Living in a minister's home my whole life has brought me up close to the worst that Christians experience. I've received crisis phone calls.

I've watched Christians drop out of church. I've witnessed ugly divorces and painful family rifts. I've known Christians who ended their own lives. These things are bewildering when you know God promises in His Word that His people can experience perpetual victory and irrepressible joy.

Equally perplexing is seeing scores of believers make great plans for serving God and extending His kingdom, yet nothing ever comes of those dreams. Despite their talk about having heard from God and having a vision for what they want to do on God's behalf, their lives seem to make little lasting difference for God's kingdom.

Numerous longtime believers continue to struggle with the same carnal and selfish habits, never experiencing victory and moving on. Joyless Christians, stubborn, unforgiving

> *Countless Christians rarely experience the depths of God's presence and promises.*

Christians, bitter Christians who claim they believe in God's power but who never experience it—you know them. Perhaps you're one of them.

In moments of candor, many believers confess that even after years of walking with Christ, they still struggle to take time to pray and to read their Bible. Even pastors, who are paid to be spiritual, regularly admit spending woefully inadequate time in prayer. Countless numbers of Christians are living their lives on the surface of what God intended for them, and they rarely experience the depths of God's presence and promises.

Then I encounter people like my father and the other men and women I've mentioned, and I realize some people *are* receiving the magnificent blessings God promised. They *are* enjoying God's presence; they *are* experiencing His power. Their lives overflow with unshakable joy. Knowing these people and witnessing their close walk with God, I wonder why so many others are satisfied with mundane, lifeless, powerless Christianity. Why don't more Christians strive to experience every truth God has pledged to them in His Word?

WE LIMIT GOD

God is the One who initiates a relationship with us, and His Holy Spirit facilitates our spiritual growth. God—limitless in His love, power, and wisdom—wants to enter into a love relationship with each of us. He's willing and eager to share His heart and thoughts with us.

We looked earlier at this astounding invitation from God: "Call to Me, and I will answer you, and show you great and mighty things, which you do not know" (Jeremiah 33:3). Consider also this invitation, equally astounding: "Draw near to God and He will draw near to you" (James 4:8). And this one from the Lord Jesus: "Come to Me, all you who labor and are heavy laden, and I will give you rest" (Matthew 11:28).

God is infinite. He can do and have whatever He wants. Yet, incredibly, He desires fellowship with finite, flawed human beings. The magnitude of His character greatly exceeds anything we can possibly comprehend. Moreover, although He has myriads of angels and heavenly creatures eager to immediately do His bidding, God still chooses to work through people. It's unfathomable. Why would God want a relationship with sinful, limited, self-centered people like us?

After many years of walking with God and seeking to go deeper with Him, I've drawn this conclusion: *We* limit God. *We* determine much of what we experience of God's power. And *we* set parameters on the depth of our relationship with God. In spite of limitless possibilities, we choose to impede what God does in our lives, so that He must say to us, "I spoke to you, rising up early and speaking, but you did not hear, and I called you, but you did not answer" (Jeremiah 7:13).

The following actions and words of Jesus merit careful attention, as they reveal certain common themes related to these limitations:

When Jesus heard it, He marveled, and said to those who followed, "Assuredly, I say to you, I have not found such great faith, not even in Israel!" (Matthew 8:10)

But He said to them, "Why are you fearful, O you of little faith?" Then He arose and rebuked the winds and the sea, and there was a great calm. (Matthew 8:26)

Then He touched their eyes, saying, "According to your faith let it be to you." (Matthew 9:29)

Now He did not do many mighty works there because of their unbelief. (Matthew 13:58)

And immediately Jesus stretched out His hand and caught him, and said to him, "O you of little faith, why did you doubt?" (Matthew 14:31)

"And whatever things you ask in prayer, believing, you will receive." (Matthew 21:22)

As soon as Jesus heard the word that was spoken, He said to the ruler of the synagogue, "Do not be afraid; only believe." (Mark 5:36)

Jesus said to him, "If you can believe, all things are possible to him who believes." Immediately the father of the child cried out and said with tears, "Lord, I believe; help my unbelief!" (Mark 9:23–24)

But Jesus looked at them and said, "With men it is impossible, but not with God; for with God all things are possible." (Mark 10:27)

"For with God nothing will be impossible." (Luke 1:37)

Then He said to the woman, "Your faith has saved you. Go in peace." (Luke 7:50)

But He said to them, "Where is your faith?" And they were afraid, and marveled, saying to one another, "Who can this be? For He commands even the winds and water, and they obey Him!" (Luke 8:25)

And He said to her, "Daughter, be of good cheer; your faith has made you well. Go in peace." (Luke 8:48)

And He said to him, "Arise, go your way. Your faith has made you well." (Luke 17:19)

But He said, "The things which are impossible with men are possible with God." (Luke 18:27)

> *We don't have to allow our limitations to hold us back from experiencing what God has for us.*

One recurring theme that jumps out from these passages is that *all* things are possible with God. Another is that people face numerous humanly impossible situations both personal and circumstantial. And another: our *faith* determines whether God will free us from our limitations.

We don't have to allow our limitations to hold us back from experiencing what God has for us. The choice is ours.

ARE YOU SATISFIED?

A disclaimer is in order here: I'm not promoting a "name it and claim it" theology. Nor is this a "health and wealth" guidebook. I do not see faith as a tool we use to get God to give us what we want.

However, I continue to meet many people who settle for mediocrity in their Christian walk. Conversely, I regularly encounter others whose vibrant spiritual life is enviable. We all serve the same God. We know He desires intimate fellowship with us. We know He wants us to experience Him in His awesome splendor. But some people allow complacency to limit their walk with Him.

If you're satisfied with your current spiritual situation, you're setting the boundaries of what you'll experience of Him. If you believe you're incapable of knowing God more intimately or of serving Him more powerfully, you're choosing to plateau spiritually.

Do you want things happening in your life that can be explained only as God's doing?

But if you sense within your soul that you've barely scratched the surface of what God has for you, if you long to go deeper with God, if you want God to use you to make a significant impact on your world, then keep reading.

Let me clarify what I mean. When I talk about God using people to make a "significant impact," I'm not necessarily referring to someone who's invited to preach a crusade in a football stadium or to address the United Nations. *Anything* God asks you to do is significant. (That's the only kind of work He does!)

What I'm asking is twofold:

First, do you want things to be happening in your life that can be explained *only* as God's doing?

Second, if God *is* doing amazing things in your life, do you want Him to do more?

Consider John Hyde's example. As a missionary in India, he asked God to bring one person to faith in Christ through his testimony *every day* for a year. God chose to answer this prayer, and Hyde daily rejoiced to see people come to Christ. Most of us would be delighted if this were our experience each year. But Hyde knew even this did not in any way exhaust what almighty God was capable of doing through the life of one of His servants. So the following year Hyde asked God for two converts per day. Once again God gave him what he asked for. Eventually Hyde was asking for, and receiving, at least five converts every day. Even then, Hyde knew God could do even greater works than that.[2]

Think about your own life. Have you grown satisfied with the present level of God's activity in and through you? Or do you long for more?

AT THE ALTAR

Several years ago my father and I spoke at a spiritual-leadership conference in Miami. I was inexperienced in leading such large meetings. My father was the headliner, and I was there as his junior apprentice.

We were to lead four sessions. I was scheduled to speak first each time, while Dad was asked to clean up my mess and close out each session. I felt pressure to keep my presentations brief because I knew everyone really wanted to hear him.

After our first session, my father surprised me. "Richard," he told me, "I sense God using you in a special way in this conference. In the next session I'd like to speak first. I'll try to be brief so you have plenty of time to share what God is laying on your heart." This meant it was up to me to extend an altar call at the close of the service.

To say the least, I felt intimidated. Sitting in the front row before me was the greatest man of God I knew. What was I doing challenging people like him to get right with God?

As I concluded my sermon, I invited people to come forward to pray and find peace with God. Immediately I noticed my father quietly making his way to a place of prayer at the front of the platform. As I saw him kneeling there, I was taken

> *I was humbled that day.*

aback. Here was the godliest man I knew, someone who was far better acquainted with God than I was. I thought, *What is* he *doing coming forward to pray after my message?*

Then the Holy Spirit said to me, *That's* why *he's such a strong Christian.*

My father has a deep hunger for God. He longs to experience God in all His dimensions. Therefore, he listens eagerly for a divine word, even when the messenger is his much-less-experienced son.

I was humbled that day, and I asked myself, "Am I willing to seek after God like that?"

'You're Not Your Dad!'

Thirteen years ago I was speaking in a church in Texas. I was a new seminary president, and I wanted to make a good impression. I knew my father had previously delivered a powerful sermon in that church, and many of the people still remembered his message. I preached my heart out.

At the close of the service, the pastor asked me to remain at the front of the auditorium so people could greet me. The congregation was gracious. Then an elderly saint approached me and peered straight in my face. "Well, son, you're good,"

> *You can't skip any of the steps.*

she said, "but you're not your dad!"

I surmised she did not have the gift of encouragement. Still holding her hand, I replied, "You're so right. Would you pray for me that one day I might become even half the man of God my father is?"

She nodded.

Then I whispered, "Can I tell you a little secret about my father?" Her eyes grew larger, and she nodded vigorously. I said, "When my dad was *my* age, he wasn't my dad either!"

Spiritual growth is a process. You can't skip any of the steps. Some things take time and prolonged effort. But there's no reason to remain where you are. There's so much God wants to reveal to you. There's so much He wants to do through you. So wherever you are in your spiritual life, I encourage you to push on to the next level.

THIS BOOK'S GOAL

I hope this book inspires you to aim for nothing less than reaching that next level. I want you to attain spiritual heights you never dreamed were possible, to experience God working through your life in a powerful new dimension, to hear words from God that will dramatically change your life and your world.

The ensuing chapters will address the most common spiritual limitations people experience, and we'll consider ways to overcome these unnecessary boundaries. I want to help you blow past every limitation you've ever set for yourself in your Christian life.

The good news is, you don't have to stay where you are. So let's get going.

Two

UNLIMITING WHAT
WE HEAR FROM GOD

After spending the first six years of married life in school, I finally completed seminary and became pastor of a church. The first two years were challenging, as my congregation had more than its share of problems. I was working as hard as I could, putting in long hours seven days a week to get my flock back on its feet.

One Saturday was a bitterly cold winter's day, and I had to do a funeral. Most of the people attending were not churchgoers, and I had no assurance the deceased (whom I'd never met) was a Christian. I spent several hours with the family trying to comfort them. Then I had to stop by my church to prepare for some special events taking place the following day.

I considered my miserable condition.

At last I could head home after a grueling day. "At least I can anticipate a warm welcome from my loving family," I mused.

Wrong. My wife's greeting was, "You forgot to take out the garbage." She'd been doing some housecleaning and had filled a large box with trash. It was blocking the hallway and was too heavy for her to carry out, so Friday night she'd asked me to remove it. Not wanting to brave the frigid night air, I promised to discard it Saturday morning on my way to the funeral. But in my haste that morning, I forgot.

Wordlessly, I grabbed the box and marched back out across the arctic tundra. Trudging back to the house like a prisoner to the scaffold, I considered my miserable condition. While most people had been enjoying their Saturday, spending leisure time with their families, I'd been away from home serving the Lord. I was depleted. I needed encouragement. But even my own family took me for granted.

Not ready to go back inside, I stood outside my house wallowing in my misery. When it's thirty degrees below zero, however, one can't prolong a pity party. You have to get right down to business! Thankfully God was prompt. He immediately reminded me of the day I first realized I wanted to marry Lisa.

WINDSHIELD MESSAGES

We were university students and had become acquainted through church events. We entered the summer as friends and had never dated each other. Lisa quickly found a summer job at a company that manufactured prefabricated buildings. She worked in the executive offices. One day she called to alert me that the warehouse where they constructed their products was opening an evening shift and needed to hire a second crew.

I was intrigued by the idea of working where she did. Although we'd never dated, I was attracted to her. She was pretty, smart, and a lot of fun. I saw the job as an excellent chance to get to know her better.

They hired me on the spot, and I concluded they had a keen eye for budding managerial talent. Actually, they were desperate for employees, as people were not eager to give up their summer evenings in exchange for such low wages. In fact, the company was so short of laborers that they had the local prison bus in low-security prisoners to work for them. This was a rough crowd. One guy my age would regularly slip out to the lumber storage area to smoke marijuana. Then he'd float back in to operate heavy machinery at the table where I worked.

The shifts were drudgery. Instead of running around with my friends enjoying the short Canadian summer, I was putting in eight and a half hours every evening with convicted felons.

Then one night at 11:30, as I was getting into my car to go home, I noticed a paper on my windshield. It looked like a ticket or a flier. It turned out to be a note from Lisa. Suddenly life seemed much brighter! I read and reread that note. The next evening there was another message. I began leaving notes on *her* windshield. I would leave her a card when I arrived in the afternoon, then find her reply when I got off work that night.

> *I gripped his throat and began to squeeze with all my might.*

Eventually it occurred on me that I could retrieve her messages during my 7:00 break each evening. As soon as the horn sounded, I would punch out my timecard and hurry out to my car to fetch Lisa's latest communiqué. I would carefully analyze her words to determine if she was starting to care for me.

I didn't notice that my drug-using colleague had observed my furtive activity. He saw every evening how quickly I punched my timecard and scurried out to the parking lot, returning a few minutes later with a big grin. He concluded I must have a generous stash of drugs in my car. And if there was a drug deal happening in the parking lot at break time, he wanted in on it.

One night this interloping inmate maneuvered himself to be the first person to check out at break time. He raced to my car and found my note from Lisa. Just as I was on my way out, he was returning to the plant, shouting to his fellow ruffians, "Look what I have!"

Fortunately he had to pass me to get back inside, and I wasn't inclined to let him go by unmolested. I lunged at him and tackled him to the gravel parking lot. A dozen of his friends, hearing the commotion, piled out of the building and surrounded us. They began stomping their feet and chanting, "Fight! Fight! Fight!" They were delighted with this unexpected entertainment.

My foe, in an effort to free both his hands to fight me, stuffed my precious letter into his mouth. I thought, *This cannot happen!* So I gripped his throat and began to squeeze with all my might. He spewed out my note. I grabbed it.

Like an epiphany, it dawned on me that he had a dozen friends surrounding me who would probably not let me just stroll away. I'm not a prophet, but at that moment I foresaw pain in my immediate future.

People have asked me, "When did you first realize Lisa was *more* to you than merely a friend?" Well, that was the moment.

Clutching that little paper, preparing myself for the worst, I knew that if the note was only from a friend, I would have readily parted with it. If it had been from my *mother,* I would have handed it over straightaway. Lisa obviously meant something special to me.

When I eventually got to read her soggy missive that night, it merely said she hoped I had a nice shift. I still have that piece of paper.

That was the memory the Holy Spirit gave me that frosty night a decade later. *So what has changed?* I asked myself. Back then I would have taken on twelve felons just to know Lisa's latest thought. If she'd expressed a hankering for ice chips found only at the peak of Mount Everest, I would have pulled on my boots and headed toward Tibet. But tonight she needed me to do something…and I became defensive and angry.

I realized the pressure and busyness of life had made me lose sight of how much I truly loved my wife. Now, instead of delighting in her words, I felt frustrated by them.

Hearing God, Loving God

Christianity is a love relationship with the person of Jesus Christ. It is not a religion to observe, a set of rituals to follow, or a list of disciplines to master. It's astounding but true that almighty God wants to communicate with us, and He has a lot to talk to us about. The same God who was present as each world empire rose and fell, who observed humanity making each scientific discovery, and who will judge every world leader, every ordinary person, and every demonic power—this God, who is infinitely wise and all-powerfully strong, wants to interact with you and me.

Too often we Christians follow the same pattern I did with Lisa. When we first met Christ, every moment with Him was exhilarating. Worshiping Him, reading our Bibles, and praying to Him brought irrepressible joy.

But then our hearts began to shift. Whereas we once eagerly rose each morning to spend time with our Savior, we begin to make the flimsiest excuses for missing our time with Him. Whereas we used to soak up eternal truths found on every page of God's Word, we begin more and more to leave our Bible unopened.

Scripture claims that when our heart turns away from God, we stop hearing from Him (Deuteronomy 30:17). Each of us must decide how closely we want to walk with God. We can choose mediocrity in our Christian life, or we can resolve to go deeper spiritually, growing in our love for God and increasing our capacity to hear from Him.

It's an intriguing phenomenon that God reveals deep truths to some people while others rarely receive a fresh or exciting divine message. Christianity is a two-way relationship between God and His people. However, some people read their Bible and pray yet hardly ever hear God speak. Others must discipline themselves and even force themselves to spend time with God so they can hear what He has to say.

> *Each of us must decide how closely we want to walk with God.*

Do you know preachers or Bible teachers who regularly share powerful scriptural insights God has given them? Isn't it inspiring to listen to these men and women teach God's Word? They illuminate profound truths you never noticed yourself. Conversely, other teachers merely skim the surface of the Scriptures, pointing out the obvious but never going deep. Why do some people enjoy a dynamic, vibrant relationship with God while others struggle with complacency?

ALL YOU CAN BEAR

John 13 introduces a powerful section of the New Testament—the account of the Last Supper. To the disciples this was little more than another Passover meal. They expected to share many more such occasions with Jesus in the future. But Jesus understood it was a final opportunity to impart truth to His closest followers before He was brutally removed from them.

After they'd eaten, and Judas had departed to betray his Master, Jesus began one of His most profound discourses. (Read chapters 13–16 in John's gospel and ponder the enormous weight of what He said.)

As Jesus spoke, He knew these men were entering the worst night of their lives. Before morning, Peter would deny any association with Jesus. The others would flee for their lives, hiding in fear from their enemies. All of them, except perhaps John, would look back with shame on that horrible night.

Jesus alone realized all this was coming. He also knew they weren't ready for the challenges they were about to face. So He taught them one last time. As He looked into the face of each disciple, Jesus wanted to prepare them all for what lay ahead. He loved them deeply, and there was so much they still needed to know. There in the upper room, He taught them one profound truth after another.

Suddenly Jesus stopped. "I still have many things to say to you," He said, *"but you cannot bear them now"* (John 16:12).

Can you imagine the disappointment the disciples must have felt? Here they were listening to some of the richest instruction ever spoken, and it was abruptly ending.

> *Jesus knew they weren't ready for what they were about to face.*

Knowing this was the last time He would speak at length to them before His crucifixion, why didn't Jesus press on and teach them more?

Jesus stopped giving His disciples any further truths because of a fundamental scriptural principle:

God will not reveal more truth to you than you're capable of receiving.

Our human minds can only handle so much. Our spiritual maturity limits us. If we have a shallow walk with God, we cannot expect to receive deep revelations from Him. God will match His words to us with our capacity to receive them.

The writer of Hebrews addressed the following words to Christians who had been believers for some time yet were still immature:

> For though by this time you ought to be teachers, you need someone to teach you again the first principles of the oracles of God; and you have come to need milk and not solid food. For everyone who partakes only of milk is unskilled in the word of righteousness, for he is a babe. But solid food belongs to those who are of full age, that is, those who by reason of use have their senses exercised to discern both good and evil. (5:12–14)

The writer chastised these believers because they enjoyed lightweight sermonettes and devotional thoughts but lacked the spiritual maturity to handle more substantial truths of the faith. The expectation is clear: believers ought to steadily mature in their faith so they're able to receive deeper and deeper words from God. If you aren't doing that…something's wrong.

GOING DEEPER?

What does it mean to "go deeper" with God?

Suppose one morning you're studying John 15. As you read, you come upon a verse that jumps out at you. You think, "Wow! Where did *this* come from? I've read this chapter many times, but these words

never stood out to me like this. Why didn't I notice earlier how profound this is?" There could be many reasons, but it might be that you
weren't in a place spiritually to handle that truth before. There was no
point in the Holy Spirit revealing the verse's deeper meaning to you
yet; you wouldn't have been prepared to properly respond to it.

Why do some people continually have "aha!" moments when reading their Bible, while others rarely do? It could be that some believers are
steadily increasing their capacity to receive truth from God, so the Holy
Spirit is regularly revealing more to them. Others are mired in the same
place spiritually, so they're hearing nothing new.

How spiritual do you have to become before there's nothing new to
learn from the Holy Scriptures? The Bible contains God's eternal truth,
so you'll never plumb its depths. God's Word holds unlimited layers of
truth that even the greatest Christian saint could never wholly fathom.
You'll never exhaust the supply of God's revelations and promises. With
so much to learn and discover, a Christian's natural response ought to be
to plunge into the Bible's pages with a hunger to know as much as
possible about the Lord and His purposes and ways.

> *Why do some people continually
> have "aha!" moments when
> reading their Bible,
> while others rarely do?*

If you don't already do so, I encourage you to make a habit of writing down (journaling) what God says to you when you read His Word.
The Lord will often speak to you today about what He knows you're
going to face tomorrow. It's therefore crucial to listen carefully and
remember what He says. Don't content yourself with generalized devotional thoughts. God speaks so you'll be prepared to navigate life successfully. The greater your capacity to hear from Him, the better
prepared you'll be to live victoriously.

What if, as you flip back the pages in your journal to last year or five years ago, you discover that God is working on the same issues with you now that He was back then? If God isn't revealing anything new to you, what might that tell you? It could mean you haven't grown. Your spiritual sluggishness requires God to repeat Himself to you.

Infinite God has so much to teach you, but you must develop the maturity to receive the wisdom He wants to impart to you.

INCREASING MY CAPACITY

When I first understood this truth, it shook me up. I realized almighty God has a heart full of truths He wants to share with me. He knows the future; He sees *my* future. He has plans for me and my wife, my children and grandchildren, my church, my nation, and my world.

God also sees my limitations—the things that hinder my readiness to receive His truths.

It broke my heart to realize God must withhold things from me because I'm unprepared to receive them. They include profound truths that are beyond my ability to grasp and might confuse or frighten me. They're things that could puff me up with pride because I lack the spiritual maturity to manage what I'm learning.

So God will reveal to me only what I'm capable of handling. At the same time, the Holy Spirit is continually at work stretching me so He can share more with me in the future.

I was not on any honor roll in high school. To be honest, I was surprised when I was accepted into university. I was so intimidated by higher learning that for my first semester, I inadvertently registered for an Introduction to Philosophy course rather than Introduction to Psychology. (Somehow I mistook the abbreviation *Phil.* for *psychology;*

spelling was never my strong suit.) The professor for this philosophy class was the head of the department. He was a German man, older and tremendously intimidating. He never smiled, and in the first class he made it clear he was proud to be an atheist.

At one point he asked a question, and a female student sitting near me attempted to answer it. She was obviously a Christian and vainly attempted to "defend" God. The professor made mincemeat of her response. He mocked her so mercilessly that she laid her head down on her desk and began to cry.

That was my first university class. I was scared! I realized I wasn't prepared to deal with the onslaught the secular university world was going to unleash on my faith. Sunday school answers would clearly be inadequate.

> *"I have been waiting
> all your life for this moment."*

When I arrived home that day, my father was sitting in the living room. I sat down beside him and began to pour out my concerns, recounting the vitriolic diatribe the philosophy professor had directed at our class. I described how he dismantled the simplistic answers of my classmate and how he'd issued an arrogant challenge to any other Christians in the class.

"Dad," I moaned, "I've never had to answer someone like that before. I need help! This could be a very long year if I don't learn how to handle people like him."

I'll never forget my dad's response. He leaned back in his chair, folded his hands behind his head, and with a huge smile spreading across his face declared, "I have been waiting all your life for this moment."

My father is highly educated and well read. He has three earned degrees and four honorary doctorates. He has read thousands of books and wrestled with deep theological and philosophical issues. There's nothing he enjoys more than a sophisticated, thought-provoking discussion. Yet all through my preschool years he'd patiently listened to me describe how I'd bravely fought against make-believe bad guys and monsters. He'd talked with me about my plans to become a fireman. He spent hours with me talking over strategy for our basketball, soccer, and softball teams. He heard all about cars I liked or my favorite NHL team's current standings. Year by year my father enjoyed having fellowship with me, talking about things that consumed my world. But in his heart he anticipated the day we would discuss the deep issues that have challenged the world's greatest minds throughout history. My father had his own thoughts and concerns, and he longed for a child who could discuss them with him.

When I came home from college that day, my dad realized I was now prepared and eager to talk with him about new and much weightier issues. Since that day, we've had many such conversations.

There was nothing wrong or sinful about a young boy wanting to discuss childish issues. My dad was happy to converse with me at every level when I was growing up. But GI Joes and my favorite hockey team were not what he spent his time contemplating. His thoughts were on a much higher plane. When I saw his delight in being able to talk philosophy with me, I think I caught a glimpse of how God feels when His children grow ready to communicate with Him about matters on His heart.

The Source of Spiritual Maturity

During the first centuries of church history, a heresy known as Gnosticism proclaimed the existence of divine mysteries that only the spiritual elect knew. It became a source of great pride to be privy to secrets of God that were hidden from the common believer. I disagree with Gnosticism.

Spiritual maturity comes not from learning secrets and gaining insider information about God's kingdom, but from walking faithfully with God and regularly obeying what He tells you.

The biblical principle is that you cannot receive meaty words until you've properly digested—and obeyed—milk words. It's a process. There's no mystery to going deeper with God in His Word. God's intention for every believer is that we continue to mature spiritually as we daily get to know Him better.

In John 16:13 Jesus spoke these words about the Holy Spirit:

> When He, the Spirit of truth, has come, He will guide you into
> all truth; for He will not speak on His own authority, but what-
> ever He hears He will speak; and He will tell you things to come.

What a wonderful promise from the Lord! Jesus did not condemn His followers for failing to be more mature. Instead He held out a promise to them: the Holy Spirit would enable the disciples to grow by sharing as much of God's Word with them as they were prepared to receive.

If you want to know how this played out in the disciples' lives, read the book of Acts. Obviously the Lord took these men a long way in their faith and knowledge of spiritual matters, and the world still feels the impact.

> *Jesus did not condemn them for failing to be more mature. Instead He held out a promise.*

Do you want to receive more profound truths from God? If you do, then obey what He's presently telling you. Obedience, not arguing, leads to spiritual growth. The closer your walk with God, the keener will be your receptivity to His Word. If you ignored the last three things God told you to do, why would He give you an exciting, deeper revelation? Instead, He'll keep bringing you back to the last thing He said until you're finally ready to respond. Sadly, some people remain in the same place spiritually because they refuse to obey what God told them years ago.

Inadequate Clichés

As a young pastor I came to realize why it was critical for me to hear a fresh word from God.

One of our faithful church members suffered from an aggressive, devastating cancer. The disease ravaged her body, but her heart was so strong it refused to stop beating.

As the pain grew unbearable, the doctors prescribed large doses of morphine. While this dulled her pain, it also caused her to become delusional. She began to express violent anger toward her husband. This godly woman, who had never said an unkind word to anyone, would scream horrible accusations at her heartbroken spouse. While this poor man was grieving at what the disease was doing to his wife, he couldn't let her see him for fear it would set her off again.

One night I received a phone call summoning me to the hospital. I entered the intensive care unit and cautiously approached the woman's bedside. She was sleeping fitfully. I looked around in that dimly lit area, but I couldn't see her husband. Finally I noticed him sitting on the floor at the foot of the bed, weeping. As I squatted beside him and looked into his face, I saw tears streaming down his cheeks. In a broken voice he asked, "Pastor, why doesn't God take her home?"

In that moment I was keenly aware that this man did not need a Christian cliché or a greeting card poem. He couldn't bear a superficial, careless answer. He desperately wanted a word from God. Several times

I began to answer, and each time the words I was preparing to utter seemed hopelessly inadequate. Finally I pulled out my Bible and began reading from Psalms. As we listened to God's Word, we were both gently reminded that God was still in control. Whether or not we understood our circumstances, God did—and that was enough.

I came away with a permanent reminder that when I give people my opinion rather than a word from God, I grossly shortchange them. People don't need me; they need God. A word from me can't change anyone. A word from God sets people free.

As a pastor I knew that the auditorium was filled every Sunday with people who desperately needed to know what God said about their situations. Some couples sat together in church yet were miles apart in their relationship. They needed to know God could heal their wounded marriage. Some parents were bewildered, not knowing how to help their struggling teenager, and they wanted to hear how God could help them. Young couples didn't see how they would make their next rent payment, and they had to understand how walking with God made a practical difference in their lives. Every time I approached the pulpit, I knew I had a unique opportunity to share God's Word and to be an instrument to set people free.

> *When I give people my opinion rather than a word from God, I grossly shortchange them.*

GOD HAS SOMETHING TO SAY

Does God have anything to say about your circumstances? Of course He does. He knows how many days you'll live on the earth (Psalm 139:16). He knows how and when you'll die. He knows every crisis as well as every temptation you'll face. And He knows how to use you for His kingdom purposes so your life reaches its maximum potential.

More than that, God has His own thoughts He's willing to share with you—like the "great and mighty things" of Jeremiah 33:3. Imagine! Infinite, omniscient God offering to reveal to us His thoughts on a matter! And all so that we as His holy servants can "do according to what is in My heart and in My mind" (1 Samuel 2:35) as He shares those things with us.

The Holy Spirit knows what's on the heart and mind of the heavenly Father, and He's prepared to dispense God's wisdom and counsel to us (1 Corinthians 2:9–16). What an unparalleled privilege! And what a great need, for we live in a day when we desperately need to know God's thoughts toward our world.

OVERCROWDED IN SINGAPORE

This past summer I had the privilege of taking my daughter with me on a speaking tour of Singapore, Malaysia, Australia, and New Zealand. Our first stop was Singapore. We arrived on the day British authorities arrested several suspected terrorists who were allegedly plotting to blow up as many as nine jetliners as they crossed the Atlantic between the United States and Britain. When Carrie and I arrived, the Singapore airport was buzzing with concerned passengers and security officials trying to determine how widespread the danger was. The world had been reminded once more of how uncertain and dangerous life can be.

That evening I was scheduled to speak on the topic "Hearing God's Voice." The venue was a beautiful thousand-seat auditorium. Our host confided to me that she was uncertain how many people would come; it was a busy weeknight, and there was no preregistration for the event.

When I arrived, the building was quickly filling up. Soon I noticed ushers putting extra chairs in the aisles and in the back. People kept coming. Finally the organizers closed the doors and told those just arriving that there was no more room.

It was a graphic reminder to me that people desperately want to know when God is speaking. We need to hear from Him. His Word is our life (see Deuteronomy 30:19–20).

While I was in Singapore, two verses from Psalm 40 stood out to me. Verse 12 says:

> For innumerable evils have surrounded me;
> My iniquities have overtaken me,
> 　　so that I am not able to look up;
> They are more than the hairs of my head;
> Therefore my heart fails me.

In light of the recent terrorist threat, I thought, Lord, the psalmist was so right. This world is filled with evil. Every time I watch the news there are more disheartening reports. Wickedness pervades our world.

Then the Lord drew my attention back to verse 5:

> Many, O LORD my God, are Your wonderful works
> Which You have done;
> And Your thoughts toward us
> Cannot be recounted to You in order;
> If I would declare and speak of them,
> They are more than can be numbered.

Evil tidings may abound, and my own shortcomings may be numerous, but God's thoughts toward me are infinite!

I was greatly encouraged to realize God's heart is filled with loving thoughts toward me. It made me want to know what He's thinking—if almighty God has heavenly thoughts toward me and my future,

People desperately want to know when God is speaking.

it's inconceivable that I wouldn't make every effort to learn what they are.

If God has more to say to me, I want to hear it.

Sermons or Messages?

As someone who has the opportunity to regularly preach and teach, I've seen the stark contrast between preaching a sermon and delivering a word from God.

When I was in seminary, my father was invited to speak at a city-wide service near my home. An acclaimed preacher was to share the platform with him that evening. I'd heard this other man preach before, and I was extremely impressed with his oratory skill. He had a booming, resonant voice, and his illustrations and storytelling were masterful. My father, on the other hand, wasn't nearly so polished a speaker. To be honest, I was somewhat concerned that Dad was a little out of his league.

That evening a massive choir sang before each sermon. After an inspiring anthem from them, the first man rose and delivered the consummate sermon. Every word had been carefully chosen. Each engaging story was meticulously crafted. I sensed that every gesture and voice inflection had been fastidiously selected and practiced. This man knew what he was doing.

At the close of his presentation, the entire congregation burst into applause. My heart sank. I thought, *My dad has to follow* that?!

As so often happens in such events, the service went long. Additional testimonies and reports took us well beyond the allotted time on the program. It grew so late, the choir was dismissed instead of singing before my father's message. When Dad got to the pulpit, the worship leader hinted that the hour was late, so he should keep his sermon brief.

My father's sermon was anything but polished. He simply shared from the overflow of his heart what God was teaching him at that time (this was while he was preparing to write *Experiencing God*).

As he drew his message to a close, I was nervous. What if no one clapped? It would be embarrassing after the enthusiastic applause the first speaker received. As my father's firstborn, I felt obligated to safeguard his honor, and I wildly entertained the thought of clapping my hands and whistling to drum up some support. But that would be too obvious.

I bowed my head and hoped for the best.

As my father sat down, there was only silence. No clapping.

Poor Dad, I thought. *Not even a halfhearted "Amen" from that entire audience!*

Then I heard a strange noise that was barely audible at first. I noticed an older man in my pew whose face was wet with tears. Then I saw that people all over that massive auditorium were weeping. It dawned on me that the worship leader hadn't dismissed the service. He was on his knees at the front of the auditorium with his head bowed, fervently praying. Others began quietly making their way to the front of the church to kneel and pray. Those in the balcony knelt beside their pews. All around me people seemed to be physically shaken by what they'd just heard.

It became clear to me what had happened. The first speaker had preached a sermon and impressed everyone with his skills. My father had delivered a message from God, and everyone was shaken by the divine encounter. The power did not come from my father's polished delivery. The other speaker was superior in that department. I knew my father had always hungered for a deep walk with God. God *had* worked in his life, and on that evening he was simply God's messenger, sharing with us what God had shared with him.

As a preacher I'm acutely aware that people in the audiences I address do not need another sermon. They need a divine message. Today in North America, more sermons are preached every week than at any other time in history. The United States and Canada are filled with churches, worship services, Christian television and radio programs, Christian books, Christian conferences, and special ministries. The land abounds with sermons. Yet the spiritual condition of North America continues to deteriorate. Jesus claimed in John 8:32 that the truth would set people free, yet despite the plethora of sermons and the technology to make them easily available, people are experiencing increasing bondage.

> *People in the audiences I address do not need another sermon. They need a divine message.*

This has created a profound sense of accountability in me. As I approach a pulpit, I ask myself, "Am I about to deliver a sermon I prepared or a message God inspired?"

I have to consider when the Holy Spirit last took me to a new level of understanding of God's Word. When did I last come out of my time with God so excited about what He said to me I could hardly wait to tell someone? When was the last time others were deeply impacted by something God said to *me*?

Eloquent words don't change lives; divine words do.

Did you know there are numerous sermon sites on the Internet? They provide complete outlines, manuscripts, and even PowerPoint presentations to purchase and download with a click of a mouse. Any guesses which day receives a glut of hits every week? Saturday, of course. Many spiritually anemic preachers are going online to find a sermon to preach to their spiritually malnourished congregations. Could that explain why people who regularly attend church are divorcing at rates similar to those who stay home to read the paper? Could that be why a steady diet of contemporary preaching is not helping believers achieve victory in their lives? Scripture promises that people will be set free, not by good sermons, but by God's truth.

NO DIFFERENCE

A pastor once approached me at the close of a conference to express his frustration. He told me he was actively looking for another church in which to serve. He went on to say his church was not a house of prayer. He told me he firmly believed in prayer, but his people refused to pray. No one attended the weekly prayer meeting. When he organized prayer conferences or prayer studies, no one showed up. He told me he didn't want to waste the remainder of his ministry on "prayerless people."

When I asked how long he'd been pastor there, he replied, "Fifteen years."

I wasn't trying to add to this man's misery, but I felt compelled to ask him, "Have you considered why it is that after fifteen years of exposure to your preaching on prayer, teaching on prayer, modeling prayer, rejoicing in answers to your prayers, and encouraging prayer, *no one* in your church is interested in prayer?"

Of course, that hadn't been his focus. The fact was that although this pastor knew prayer was important, he'd apparently not been sharing God's heart on the subject. In fact, the pastor obviously didn't believe in prayer himself, since he'd quit praying for his people and now was looking for a more spiritual congregation in which to serve.

The truth is, if no one is responding to what you have to say, that may indicate it's *your* message, not God's, that you're delivering.

You may be thinking, *Yes, but didn't people reject God's prophets too? And* they *had a message from God!* Excellent point. Scripture indicates that God's Word never returns to Him without having accomplished His purposes (Isaiah 55:10–11). This doesn't mean people will always *accept* and *obey* God's message; people in biblical times often rejected God's prophets. However, they could not remain indifferent to a word from God. Either they accepted it, or they rejected it and stood in judgment before it. God's

> *If no one's responding, maybe you're delivering* your *message, not God's.*

Word vindicated itself. A word from God always came to pass (see Deuteronomy 18:21–22).

Furthermore, prophets who knew that their message came from God did not generally cease delivering it. Jeremiah certainly was tempted to quit. After all, forty years of rejection can demoralize the most enthusiastic messenger! Yet whenever Jeremiah began to face discouragement, he received a fresh word from God that renewed his vigor. Jeremiah didn't quit delivering his unpopular message, because he knew it came from God

HAVING WHAT OTHERS NEED

When there's a limit to what we hear from God, it's a limit we have chosen ourselves.

Are you satisfied with your present spiritual condition? Do you care if you hear more of God's thoughts about your life, your family, and your world? By accepting limits in our life, we are also

> *I cannot dole out*
> *superficial answers and platitudes*
> *to my children's serious life challenges.*

limiting the extent God will bless others through us. We can't give to others what we don't have ourselves.

I have three young-adult children. They're entering a dangerous, confusing, evil world. They need a word from God. They need parents who have a word from God to dispense. I can't give them something I don't have. I cannot be content to merely dole out superficial answers and platitudes to my children's serious life challenges.

When my wife and I face difficult situations, I want the Lord to entrust me with His deepest thoughts on these issues. I want to be firmly planted in God's Word so I have solid, wise insight to give to my family and to those who look to me for answers. They rely on their parents to have a word from God to dispense. They should have God's best, so I need to know what that is.

THE CHALLENGE

I want to challenge you about your current walk with God. As wonderful and fulfilling as it may be, I promise you there's still far more of God to know and to experience. As awesome as your times with God may be right now, I pray you'll continually grow in your capacity to receive more from Him. In what I'm able to hear from God, I don't want to be just as limited this year as I was last year. I want to grow.

You may be discouraged with your spiritual life. You may have tried and tried to have meaningful quiet times and to pray, but it always deteriorates into drudgery. Let me encourage you: it really doesn't have to be that way. Perhaps you're like the Israelites in the wilderness and have been going in circles for years. That's tedious. Spend time with God and ask Him to do whatever is necessary in you so you can reach a new place spiritually with Him. He wants to take you there.

God has a lot to talk with you about. Are you prepared to pay the price so you can hear what He has to say? Are you ready to receive a deeper word from God than you've ever heard before?

If so, get ready. A word from God will change your life.

QUESTIONS FOR REFLECTION

1. List the last three things you clearly know God said to you. If possible, put a date beside them. How did you respond?
2. Are you presently enjoying your times alone with God? What do you think you need to adjust so you experience more from these times?
3. Would you describe your current spiritual condition as feeding on the milk or the meat of God's Word? What would it take for you to go to the next level with God?
4. If you're a Bible teacher or someone who shares counsel and encouragement with others, how would you describe the depth of your teaching? How are people responding to what you share with them?

THREE

UNLIMITING GOD'S WORK
THROUGH US

As soon as I became pastor of my first church, I saw there was much to do. The church had been on a plateau or in decline for seven years. People were discouraged. In my youthful enthusiasm, I planned several special events. For example, I brought in a guest speaker to do a series of meetings. The response to these meetings filled an auditorium that had not been full for years. Several people became Christians. God's Spirit was evident.

A couple of weeks later, on the Monday before Easter, the church council met to plan and evaluate how things were going. I anticipated an uplifting time as these leaders discussed what a great job I was doing as pastor. I imagined their effusive gratitude: "Richard, you've been here only a few months, and already we're beginning to fill up the building." "Richard, you're so young, and yet God is using you so mightily." "You're the best pastor we've ever had!" Then I would humbly bow my head, close my eyes, and point heavenward.

I was way off.

CRITICIZED TO A WHOLE NEW LEVEL

As the meeting commenced, a disgruntled council member launched into a litany of complaints about how the meetings had been conducted. There should have been better advertising, she said. There could have been more effective follow-up. More people ought to have been informed and involved. Who was making all the decisions anyway?

On and on it went. Most of the others kept their eyes lowered and didn't say a word.

When I arrived home, my phone was already ringing. People who had been in the meeting were calling to plead with me not to resign because of the tongue-lashing. They assured me they didn't share the opinions of that outspoken council member. When I asked why they hadn't spoken up during the meeting, they all confessed they didn't want to become the woman's next victim. After all, they pointed out, I was paid to deal with people like that.

Later that week, the plot thickened as I made one of my many rookie pastor mistakes. Normally a group of us would meet at 6:30 on Friday mornings to pray, followed by breakfast together. Since it was Good Friday that week, I decided to cancel the prayer time so everyone could sleep in and have breakfast at home with their families. Unfortunately I made the decision at the last minute. On Thursday evening I called everyone who normally attended to inform them it was canceled.

Later I felt guilty about canceling the prayer time, so on Friday I got up at 6:30 a.m. to pray at home. At 6:35 the phone rang. It was my critic from Monday evening. She'd chosen this Friday to attend the prayer meeting for her first time. Because she hadn't come before, I hadn't called her to tell her it was canceled.

"Where is everybody?" she angrily asked. "Who decided to cancel the prayer meeting? What kind of communication do we have in this church where only special people are told what's going on? What if a visitor had decided to come today and found the church locked up?" she droned on.

By the time I hung up I was miserable. As the pastor, I was work-ing as hard as I knew how. Sure, I was making mistakes, but I wasn't a bad person, and I certainly didn't deserve such abuse.

I poured out my sorrows to my wife. "What should I do?" I asked.

She thought for a moment. "Well, your parents will be here on Sunday. Maybe you should invite this lady and her family for Easter lunch."

I was flabbergasted. "Lisa, you aren't listening to me! This woman *hates* me! She thinks I'm the worst pastor who ever lived. She thinks I make Judas look like an exemplary disciple. This will be the first time my parents have visited my church. Why would I invite my worst critic to ruin my day? She'll probably critique my table etiquette!"

Lisa pondered my concerns. "What are you preaching on this Sunday?"

"It's Easter," I replied. "I'm preaching on forgiveness."

> *Sure, I made mistakes, but I certainly didn't deserve such abuse.*

She smiled wryly. "Maybe God wants you to practice it as well as preach it."

She had me. "Do you want to call her?" I asked.

"Hey, you're the pastor!"

When I called the woman, the chill over the phone line was palpa-ble. I extended my invitation, and I think she almost fainted from shock. Sounding bewildered, she agreed to come.

What I hadn't anticipated was the church's active grapevine. All my leaders had heard this woman mistreat me at the council meeting. Everyone wondered how I would respond. Would the pastor publicly shun her in the church lobby? Would he call a special meeting of the deacons to discuss disciplinary proceedings? Would he make veiled references to her in his sermons: "Beware the wolves among the sheep!"?

Then the news began making the rounds: "He invited her and her family over for Easter dinner! He must be planning to poison her!" It seemed unbelievable.

I had an unforgettable experience that Easter. I'd prepared a message on forgiveness. It was exegetically sound. The illustrations were interesting. My application was practical. But God wanted me to do more than merely preach a sermon to the people that day. He wanted me to incarnate a message. He wanted His people to *see* forgiveness in their pastor's life.

As I approached the pulpit, I sensed an authority and anointing from God I'd never experienced before. Only after God did a work in me did I have something worth sharing with people.

I discovered later that this woman had a difficult past. She'd been hurt by many of the male authority figures in her life, including former pastors. Her experience predisposed her to assume I would disappoint her as well. Only this time she was going to fire the first shot.

She needed to experience love and forgiveness. Over time,

> *God wanted His people to* see *forgiveness in their pastor's life.*

she became a great encouragement and support to me and a joy to have in the congregation.

She wasn't the only one whose trust I had to earn. Events had taken their toll on all the church members. They were wounded and wary of being hurt again. They'd heard numerous sermons, but they hadn't seen many. They needed a pastor who could rise above the petty behavior of others to model Christ to them. I hadn't been prepared to be that kind of pastor when I arrived, so God worked on me first. As God fashioned my life, I became capable of greater compassion and patience than ever before. God increased my capacity to serve Him, and I was able to bless others. What a privilege!

OVERESTIMATED

Is it possible to overestimate your ability to serve God? Certainly.

After seven years of seminary training, I thought I was ready to take on any church. But I was wrong. I still had much growing to do. Some issues in my life needed to be resolved.

It's a comfort to know the twelve disciples of Jesus were a lot like me. Even after spending three years ministering with Him, they were unprepared for some of the tasks lying before them.

Read Peter's story:

> Simon Peter said to Him, "Lord, where are You going?" Jesus answered him, "Where I am going you cannot follow Me now, but you shall follow Me afterward."
>
> Peter said to Him, "Lord, why can I not follow You now? I will lay down my life for Your sake."
>
> Jesus answered him, "Will you lay down your life for My sake? Most assuredly, I say to you, the rooster shall not crow till you have denied Me three times. (John 13:36–38)

This was the night Jesus would be arrested and crucified. He was about to undertake the greatest assignment God would ever give anyone on earth. It was a mind-boggling task of staggering proportions.

As the evening wore on, Peter realized something major was about to happen. Jesus spoke ominously of how He wouldn't be with them much longer.

Having undertaken the role of unofficial leader of the twelve disciples, Peter was the most outspoken of the group, and he also considered himself the most trustworthy (see Matthew 26:33). He'd "left all" to follow Jesus (Luke 18:28), gambling his entire career on Jesus and the kingdom He was going to establish. If Jesus was about to undertake a great work that evening, Peter intended to be at His side.

Then came those devastating words: *"Where I am going you cannot follow Me now."* Jesus knew that in spite of Peter's sincere zeal, he wasn't ready for such an immense undertaking.

From this we can glean a second principle:

God will match His assignments with your character and your walk with Him.

God doesn't grant large assignments to small characters. The depth of your walk with God is foundational to your service for Him. Peter assumed he was capable of going wherever Jesus went—after all, he'd been one of the first disciples Jesus had chosen (Mark 1:16–18), and he'd already made great sacrifices to follow his Teacher. As Jesus spoke that evening about going away, Peter may have

> *God sees your potential just as clearly as He sees where you are right now.*

recognized this as his opportunity to prove his allegiance to Jesus. However, he grossly overestimated his ability to serve God. His enthusiasm for the task was high, but his walk with God was not yet strong enough.

Peter had no idea he was still so unprepared to go on with Jesus. But Jesus knew Peter would experience dismal failure before the night was over. Despite his exuberant claims of loyalty, Peter would adamantly disassociate himself from his Master.

I'm glad that along with Jesus's candor that evening about Peter's present spiritual condition, He also offered hope: "Where I am going you cannot follow Me now, but *you shall follow Me afterward*."

The day *would* come when Peter would fulfill his vow and willingly lay down his life for his Lord. In the meantime he had a lot of maturing to do. The Lord intended to walk with Peter through that awful night to build his faith and to strengthen his resolve.

Does it encourage you to know that God sees your potential just as clearly as He sees where you are right now? God knows how to build character. He understands how to develop faith. He wants your life to fulfill its potential as He works in you and uses your circumstances to expand your capacity to serve Him.

Giving God Your Career

I can be a lot like Peter. Sometimes I too overestimate my capacity to serve God. That's why I've entrusted my life and career to the Lord. He knows far better than I do when I'm ready for another assignment or challenge. He recognizes when I've been faithful in a little and when I'm ready for Him to trust me with more.

Over the years I've known many people who were frustrated when others didn't help them advance in their careers. Pastors accused denominational leaders of passing them over for denominational positions. Middle managers blamed upper management for their lack of progress up the corporate ladder. Business people condemned the government or the economy for their business woes. Seeing this victimlike attitude has always bothered me, so as a young man I asked God to help me trust Him for whatever happened in my life. I knew God would never give me more than my character could handle.

One decision I made early on was to never lobby for a position. For me, this included never applying for a job unless I was asked to do so. I'm not saying everyone should follow this practice, but for me I felt it would remove any distraction of constantly looking on the horizon for a better job. And it could stifle the temptation to politicize my way into a career or enlist my friends to recommend me for more prominent positions. So I made a covenant with God that I would never seek a job or ministry opportunity. I've worked with people who manipulated their way into positions too big for their character, and it's highly frustrating to have a boss like that. I concluded it was far wiser to invite God to be the director of my career. He knows my capabilities far better than I do. He can initiate changes in my life anytime He sees I'm ready.

I sometimes lack confidence. Some things I would never attempt if God did not make me do it. When I was a teenager, my mother, without my knowledge, signed me up on a basketball team, then chased me out of the house with a broom so I would attend my first practice. I grew to love basketball and was

> *I made a covenant with God that I would never seek a job or ministry opportunity.*

grateful the Lord used my dear mother and her broom to introduce this new dimension into my life. Sometimes I need to take on a new challenge, but I'm unsure whether I have what it takes. In those times God will bring me a new opportunity, and regardless of whether I feel adequate for the task, I trust He knows what He's doing.

As I look back over the last twenty-five years, I'm amazed at what the Lord has done in my career. Not in my wildest dreams could I have imagined the exciting journey God had for me. I know without a doubt that if I'd been "master of my own destiny," I'd have missed out on an amazing adventure.

REVIVAL?

Not long ago I was in a meeting with some sincere Christians who longed for God to bring revival to their church and to their nation. They prayed fervently for God to turn His people back to Him and to work powerfully across the country. I was in agreement with everything they prayed.

> *What if, when revival came, we were distracted or filled with pride or in the midst of a broken relationship?*

Suddenly I had a troubling thought. Each of us assumed that when God answered our prayers and performed a mighty work, He would include *us* in His activity. Because we earnestly wanted God to bring revival, we concluded He would have a role for each of us when that revival came. But what if we weren't ready? What if, when God began to renew His people, we were distracted or filled with pride or in the midst of a broken relationship? What if, when God finally answered our prayers, we weren't prepared to be a part of His answer? After all, history shows that when God has brought revival to His people, the religious leaders were often the ones unprepared for His coming. The very ones who had prayed for God to come were so disconnected from Him when He did so that they missed out on His great work.

In that moment, as I prayed with these fellow believers, the Holy Spirit gently warned me that just because I want God to do something doesn't mean I'm prepared to be part of His answer.

Peter discovered the same thing. Though he'd longed for the Messiah to come, Peter was unprepared to participate in the greatest work the Messiah would undertake. At the climax of Jesus's mission, Peter would deny he even knew Him. Peter grossly overestimated his ability to serve God.

MUCH

If I were to define my philosophy of ministry, I would put it this way: *be faithful in a little* (see Matthew 25:21, 23; Luke 16:10; 19:17).

Scripture proves that God works sequentially in people's lives. Everyone begins as a spiritual infant. Unlike the growth of physical babies, however, our growth rate depends in large part on us.

God begins by giving each of us a "little." Perhaps once we become Christians God makes it clear He wants us to be baptized and to join a local congregation. So we do. Then God speaks to us about reading our

> *Each time we obey, we mature spiritually.*

Bible each day and spending time praying to Him. We find that enjoyable. Then God talks to us about tithing. We might squirm a little, but as we begin giving our money to the Lord, He blesses us, and we receive great joy from our investment in God's kingdom. Then God leads us to share our faith with a colleague. That pushes us firmly out of our comfort zone! We feel inadequate. We fear our friend may belittle our new faith, but we gather our courage. In a faltering, unpolished attempt, we share our convictions, and we're surprised by our co-worker's positive response.

Over the next few years, God continues to give us larger and larger assignments. Each time we obey, we mature spiritually.

This process is meant to continue the rest of our lives. We never exhaust God's will for us. There's no limit to what He can do in and through us. Those who faithfully obey each new assignment eventually discover God doing amazing things through their lives. When you ask such people how they're accomplishing so much, they'll tell you it's been a process. They started out spiritually immature; then step by step—as they remained faithful in a little—God expanded what He did through them.

But many Christians do not remain faithful. In their haste to bypass this process, they extend their reach beyond their capability.

Their attitude reminds me of something said by my younger son, Daniel, when he was fourteen. His older brother had a job in a fast-food restaurant. Dan, who's always ready with a quick retort, was asked when *he* might apply to flip burgers too. His response: "Oh, I think I'll just skip that menial stuff and go straight into upper management." As tongue-in-cheek (I hope) as that was, it's sadly reflective of the way many Christians think. As a seminary president, I heard this attitude played out often (as in, "I won't take a turn in the nursery, but I'm available to preach!").

Saying no to God, no matter how small the task, is a sure way to suspend the growth process. Of course, rather than a straight-out no, some people simply procrastinate—which isn't as abrupt but is equally defiant. Or some merely give lip service to obedience, affirming the rightness of what God requires, yet staying put. Others make excuses about how inadequate they are to obey what God is telling them. However it's packaged, when you say no to God, you cease to mature spiritually.

Perhaps you've been growing in leaps and bounds as you've obeyed each command God has given you. Then one day God says, "It's time you were reconciled with that friend who has been estranged from you the last two years."

A cold chill passes through you. It was fine obeying God when obedience meant going to exciting church services or participating in international mission trips. But this is different. Every time you think of that person who betrayed you and hurt you so deeply, you become angry. You did nothing wrong; *he's* the one who should apologize and seek reconciliation.

Yet God's prompting is clear: He's asking you to repair the damaged relationship, though you can't imagine even having a civil conversation with this person unless he firsts asks your forgiveness. Besides, for two years you've been hurting because of what he did, while he seems to be doing just fine. It doesn't seem fair.

But God persists.

This is your moment of truth. Either you obey and go forward with God, or you disobey and immediately begin to stagnate and decline spiritually.

There is no neutrality with God. There's no fence sitting. Excuses don't wash. At this point, it doesn't matter if you've been meticulously faithful in a dozen other things God asked you to do in the past. You cannot live on yesterday's obedience. Your continued spiritual growth hinges on what you do *now.*

Suppose you refuse to forgive the person who hurt you. To yourself and to your friends, you rationalize this response. But God sees your heart. You stop advancing spiritually. The joy you had in the Lord begins to fade. You may keep attending church and doing your Bible readings, and others may still consider you a strong Christian. Yet you've stopped growing. You could remain in spiritual limbo for the rest of your life, living on your reputation of previous obedience, but you'll never experience the dynamic spiritual life you could have known.

STRETCHING YOU

If God bases His assignments to you on your character and your walk with Him, how does He build your character and your faith?

> *Spiritual growth often comes when you face criticism, health problems, or financial hardship.*

There's no one particular way God helps you grow, but one thing you can count on: however He does it, there will be growing pains.

When have you matured the most in your Christian life? Was it when everything was going your way, or when you were facing crises and hardship? Inevitably people say it's through their suffering that they grow the most spiritually. That being so, what should you expect when you pray and ask God to increase your faith and to make you more like Christ?

Be prepared. Spiritual growth often comes when you face criticism, health problems, or financial hardship.

Yet here's a pattern Christians typically follow: First, we pray and ask God to make us more like Christ. Second, God allows a stretching circumstance into our lives so we can grow. Third, we call our church prayer ministry and frantically enlist everyone to pray that the latest difficulty in our life be immediately removed! I believe many of the items found on church prayer lists are actually circumstances God allowed in order to mature His people.

The reality is we must decide whether we want comfort or Christlikeness. We often can't have both.

It was when I experienced an extended period of attacks and unfair criticism from fellow Christians that God stretched me. He built some qualities in my life that I lacked. The absence of these character traits had been holding me back from greater service to God.

God knows what He can do through your life if you're willing to open yourself up to Him. He'll remove obstacles such as pride, fear, and greed that hinder your spiritual growth. Then He'll build in qualities such as humility, forgiveness, and faith.

The question is, are you satisfied with your present state of service to God? Or are you open to growth—even when it's painful?

Stretched in the Graveyard Hours

When my son Daniel was fifteen, he began experiencing severe sleep issues. He'd be awake most nights until at least 4:00 a.m. He endured periods where he was conscious seventy-two hours straight.

The hardest thing for him was the loneliness. He had to spend hours alone every night while his family and friends were sleeping.

As concerned parents, we took Daniel to various doctors and sleep clinics. We tried every remedy the doctors suggested. But his condition only worsened.

One night, unbeknown to us, Daniel hit a low point. He looked at the clock and saw it was 3:00 a.m. Knowing this would be another all-nighter, he cried out to God: "Don't You care about me? Don't You know what I'm going through? Why do You answer prayers for my friends and family but not my prayers for sleep? God, if You care about what I'm going through, I need to know—and I need to know soon." Daniel spent the remainder of the night restless and awake.

Two days later a letter came in the mail addressed to him. He was intrigued, since his mail was normally electronic. Moreover, the return address was from just down the street. The note was from a friend in his youth group. She explained that she'd suddenly been awakened in the night with a powerful burden for him, so she got up from bed to write to him. She thought about telephoning, but she feared it was too late, even for Daniel.

In her note she quoted Matthew 11:28, where Jesus said, "Come to Me, all you who labor and are heavy laden, and I will give you rest." She assured Daniel that God loved him and had special plans for his life.

She concluded by saying that what she was writing might not make sense to Daniel, but she knew she couldn't go back to sleep until she wrote to him.

Daniel was so shaken by the message, he ran with the letter all the way to her house. "When did you write this?" he asked.

Her answer revealed that it was the same night Daniel cried out to God.

"What time was it?" he persisted.

> "God, if You care about what I'm going through, I need to know…"

She told him it was 3:00 a.m.; she remembered looking at her clock and deciding it was too late to call.

So God had heard the desperate cries of a sleepless teenager in the middle of the night…and sent him a message.

My son now believed God loved him and was aware of his problem, but he had no idea why God was allowing him to go through such a frustrating experience. At least, he didn't understand until several months later.

Daniel's youth group went to summer camp. It had been a difficult year, and many of the teens had been struggling. One evening the youth pastor gathered the teenagers from our church and had them share what was happening in their lives.

When it was Daniel's turn, he told about his ongoing frustration over his inability to sleep. Then a girl spoke up. She shared how she'd undergone an extremely grueling year. She was adjusting to a blended family. She'd experienced a painful breakup with her boyfriend, had fallen into the wrong crowd at school, and was doing things she knew were wrong. It seemed that everything in her world was coming apart and she didn't fit in anywhere.

Late one night, she returned from a party feeling terribly discouraged. She felt like a failure and a disappointment to her parents. She grew obsessed with the thought that if she were to take her life, she would no longer have to struggle with the problems that plagued her. Her mind raced as she considered how easily and quickly she could end all her troubles. She grew frightened at what was happening to her. She feared she might actually commit suicide in the next few moments. It was as though her mind and body were being hijacked by an evil force intent on making her kill herself.

She desperately needed to talk to someone to stop her rapid spiral into suicide. She knew her mother was asleep, and she feared that waking her would only result in another argument. Her youth pastor would be in bed. Her best friend would be asleep.

In desperation she logged on to MSN and found one person still online: Daniel Blackaby. Because it was so late, she assumed he had simply forgotten to log out before going to bed, but she sent him a brief note. He answered immediately. "What's going on?"

She and Daniel were not close friends; they were merely acquaintances in their large youth group. But she was desperate. She told Daniel about the sinister thoughts flooding her mind. Daniel shared how he, too, had been bewildered at what was happening in his life but had come to understand that God loved him and had a purpose for him he did not yet fully understand. By the time they finished talking, she no longer felt the urge to take her life.

She concluded the story she told the youth group at camp that summer evening by saying, "If Daniel hadn't been awake that night, I would be dead today."

Then a teenage boy spoke up. He shared how he, too, had experienced a terribly difficult year. He felt as if he didn't belong anywhere. He'd become involved with a drug dealer at his high school. His life was self-destructing. Finally he decided to end it. He set a date and time when he would slash his wrist and end his misery.

When the fateful morning arrived, he arose at 4:00 a.m. and strapped ice packs to his left wrist. He wanted to numb it first to dull the pain before he cut his veins. As he waited those last few minutes, he was struck by the pathetic way his life was ending. He hadn't said good-bye to his friends. Soon he would be gone without having spoken to anyone. He decided he should talk to at least one person before he died so someone knew why he had taken his life, but he was unsure who to call at that hour.

He suddenly thought of Daniel. He knew of Daniel's sleep problems and thought there might be a chance he was having another all-nighter. He phoned, and Daniel answered on the first ring. By the time they hung up, he knew he couldn't take his life.

"If Daniel hadn't been awake that night, I'd be dead today," he concluded.

Then four other people shared how Daniel's pilgrimage and suffering had inspired them as they faced adversity that year.

At the end of that week I went to our church to greet the bus as it returned from youth camp. As soon as I saw Daniel, I knew something special had happened. He glowed.

He told me he used to believe his sleep problems were a curse, but now he realized God had used his weakest moment to do one of His greatest works. It had been an unusually difficult year in the youth group, with suicidal thoughts raging out of control. In the midst of it, God had given my son an assignment involving life and death.

Daniel beamed as he told me, "When God knew there were lives hanging in the balance, He didn't use the pastor. He didn't call on the youth leader. He called on me! He gave me a late-night ministry."

God's plans for Daniel far exceeded Daniel's own expectations. He'd been asking for a good night's sleep; God wanted to use him to save lives. Though it was physically demanding, God had moved him to a new level spiritually.

Daniel would never view his life the same way, now that he knew what God was capable of doing through him. After that difficult period in his youth group, Daniel's sleep gradually began to improve.

> God had given my son an assignment involving life and death.

Many of us, when God begins to stretch us, become consumed with the pain and miss the work He's doing in us. God never squanders our pain. When you go through a difficult experience, remember that God is still sovereign and He continues to love you. If He's allowing you to suffer, He has a reason for it. One of those purposes is always that you'll grow personally in knowing Him better.

STUCK IN CAPERNAUM

One of the most insidious hindrances to our growth is success. Jesus faced this obstacle early in His ministry.

Jesus had launched an extremely successful ministry in Galilee. Among those whom He healed in the town of Capernaum—the home-town of the fishermen Peter, Andrew, James, and John—was Peter's mother-in-law, who lay sick with a fever. "And they told Him about her at once. So He came and took her by the hand and lifted her up, and immediately the fever left her" (Mark 1:30–31).

Word quickly spread that a great healer was in the city. Soon the entire town was clamoring for His services:

> At evening, when the sun had set, they brought to Him all who
> were sick and those who were demon-possessed. And the whole
> city was gathered together at the door. Then He healed many
> who were sick with various diseases, and cast out many demons.
> (Mark 1:32–34)

All evening Jesus ministered to the crowds.

Then, as now, people associated crowds with success, and the disciples must have been relieved to see Him becoming so popular so fast. After all, they'd left their fishing careers to follow this itinerant teacher.

Jesus had quickly made His mark. Perhaps as Peter, Andrew, James, and John drifted off to sleep later that night, they speculated how perfect Capernaum would be as a base of operations for their ministry with Jesus. Here their Master was accepted and successful. It would be a good life. He could remain in Capernaum for years and enjoy the benefits of being its most celebrated healer and teacher. His ministry would draw crowds from far and wide, for everyone who needed Him would know where to find Him.

Early the next day the crowds were already gathering again. Peter was eager to give the people what they'd come for. But Jesus wasn't around.

> Now in the morning, having risen a long while before daylight, He went out and departed to a solitary place; and there He prayed. And Simon and those who were with Him searched for Him. When they found Him, they said to Him, "Everyone is looking for You."
>
> But He said to them, "Let us go into the next towns, that I may preach there also, because for this purpose I have come forth." (Mark 1:35–38)

With plenty of compelling reasons to remain in the place of His success, Jesus had risen early the next morning to pray and spend time with the heavenly Father. His ministry would not be determined by practical considerations, or by issues of safety, success, or popularity, but by His Father's will. Jesus knew that His initial success in Capernaum didn't mean He was supposed to settle into a local ministry there.

Jesus wasn't around.

By the time Peter found Him, Jesus knew what His Father wanted for Him next. He had confirmed His Father's will for His life through His prayer time earlier that morning. He needed to keep moving.

And after explaining this to Peter, Jesus continued to minister "throughout all Galilee" (Mark 1:39).

Early success can prove to be a dangerous pitfall for Christians. They're faithful to do what God tells them, so God blesses them. Well-meaning friends immediately proclaim, "You've found your niche! You've discovered your spiritual gift! You're indispensable!" The great temptation for those hearing such accolades is to assume they've "arrived." Understandably, people want to invest their lives in successful ventures that bring praise and affirmation.

The problem is that we can wrongly attribute our success to our current situation. God can and will work through us anytime and anywhere. It's crucial for us to realize that God wants us to grow in our personhood and in our walk with Him. We will never totally arrive; there are always more areas for growth. There's always more of Him to know and experience. For this reason, He'll lead us to places we would never choose ourselves.

Some people find their Capernaum too early in life. When I attended seminary, I met people who had sensed God calling them into Christian ministry and had come to seminary to prepare for God's assignment. While there, they started a company to earn enough money to pay for tuition and living expenses. Their business became so successful they were still doing it a decade later, never having finished seminary or gone into ministry as God had instructed them.

Others take a job and experience some success. Later, as they realize they've outgrown their current job, they cannot bring themselves to uproot their family and move to a new city where a more challenging and rewarding career could be found.

Professors eagerly take on a new teaching role but, after decades of teaching the same material, find themselves merely going through the motions—and their students pay the price. A businesswoman achieves a national position but never considers how God might be preparing her for international influence. A surgeon achieves a coveted position at a prestigious hospital and settles

> *It is wrong to stop growing.*

into a comfortable life, forgetting his earlier dream of doing medical missions.

Some people obtain a job in their hometown and settle down to raise a family and to build their retirement income. Over time they become respected and loved by their community, but their spiritual life is no deeper or richer than it was a decade earlier. They know their job so well they don't feel challenged by it anymore. God provides them with exciting new opportunities, but they've become too ensconced in their comfortable, predictable lifestyle to respond.

Having settled in for the long haul, countless people have not experienced a fresh new growth opportunity in years. They died a long time ago but haven't yet scheduled the funeral.

Let me emphasize that it isn't a sin to stay in the same job or occupation for an extended period of time. But it is wrong to stop growing.

SEMINARY COMFORT

When I was a college student, God clearly called me to follow Him to seminary and to prepare my life for ministry. I assumed God wanted me to be pastor of a church for the rest of my life. I couldn't imagine anything I would rather do.

For four years I thoroughly enjoyed being a pastor. Over time, our congregation began to grow. We paid off the church's building mortgage early. We added staff members. My aptitudes and skills seemed to match my calling perfectly, and the people loved me (or at least they faked it well!). And we were in a great community for raising our children.

Then I received a phone call that changed my life. I was invited to become the second president of the Canadian Southern Baptist Seminary in Cochrane, Alberta, Canada. This new position gave me the opportunity to impact people's lives as they prepared to serve in Christian ministry around the world. It allowed me to speak in churches and at conferences across North America. The trustees told me they wanted a president who had been a successful pastor in Canada and who could be a role model for those who were training to do the same. I realized that being a pastor wasn't the final stop for me; it was preparatory for what God wanted to do next through my life. I agreed to move to Cochrane.

> *I've been asked to do things that would have seemed like a dream only a few years earlier.*

For the next thirteen years I served as president of a growing seminary, and they were rewarding years. Over time I acquired a godly, dedicated faculty and staff. The students were wonderful. I enjoyed a tremendous relationship with the school's trustees, who were all highly supportive and affirming. It became rare for me to hear criticisms of my performance (even when there was ample fodder for doing so). My family loved our town and the life we'd developed. Everything indicated that I'd found my niche and I should spend the rest of my working days leading this fine school.

But I'd also started to become comfortable in a routine. Though there was still much work to be done, in my heart I didn't have the same passion and vision for the work that I once had.

Then God chose to introduce a dramatic change. One day I had a fateful conversation. An alumnus came by to share what he sensed God doing in my life. When he finished, I knew without a doubt God was calling me to something new. I had certainly not been looking for a new job. (As I mentioned earlier, my attitude has always been this: be faithful where God has placed you, and don't go seeking greener grass.) Yet suddenly God had intervened and made it clear He once again had an entirely different assignment for me.

That new assignment would bring the privilege of working more closely than ever with my father. Over the years, I'd written numerous books with him, and we'd spoken together in many conferences. God was telling me to leave the seminary and work full time for Blackaby Ministries International (BMI), the ministry my father founded after retiring from a position with his denominational mission board. Quitting my job as a seminary president to work with someone who had been retired for six years didn't seem like a wise career move, but that's what God was telling me to do.

So this past year was a transition time for me. Even now, if I try to anticipate what my future working for BMI will look like or if I consider how financially secure I'll be in five years, I end up with a lot more questions than answers. But the opportunities God has given me since I made the switch have been incredible. In my new position I'm being pushed and stretched in ways I've never experienced. I've been asked to do things that would have seemed like a dream only a few years earlier. It's exhilarating to follow the Lord!

God is growing me. The church and the seminary were both challenging places to serve; God used those ministries to build certain things into my life. Then, once I grew, God put me in a new situation where I could develop in other ways.

I've come to realize that everything God asks you to do is preparation for an even bigger assignment. You never retire from your Christian growth! If you become comfortable and highly successful at what you do, perhaps God is preparing to add a new dimension to your life. If He is—be ready to respond.

STUNTED

In a world so desperate for strong Christian leaders in churches, business, politics, medicine, education, and other fields, why is there such a woeful shortage of people who are making a dramatic impact for God's kingdom?

Is it that God cannot raise up more of His followers to achieve greater things? Of course not.

I believe it's because too many Christians have become satisfied with where they are right now. They've grown comfortable and complacent. They assume they've already reached their potential, and they've forgotten they're on a journey. They stopped obeying, so they quit growing. They quit growing, and the world has gone wanting.

> *You must be willing to break through your present boundaries.*

God might not lead you to a career change, but you can be certain He intends for you to keep growing. Perhaps you're a successful physician; God may call you to take international mission trips to use your skills for His kingdom. You may be a prosperous businessperson; God may not ask you to change your career, but He may want you to join a prison ministry or teach a youth Sunday school class or write a book. God may ask you to learn another language so you can minister to the migrant workers who pass through your town every summer. He may call you to take seminary classes to enhance your Bible teaching at your local church.

There are countless ways God can develop you, but you must be willing to break through your present boundaries.

Limited by Pride

As a child, I dreamed of the day I would be a pastor. When I finally became one, I enthusiastically undertook my new responsibilities. I arose at five every morning and spent hours studying God's Word and crafting the best sermons I could. I gave attention to every administrative detail of the church. I

> *The problem with asking God a hard question is that He may give you a hard answer.*

recruited people to serve in our various ministries. I attended countless meetings. I worked as hard as I could, and I saw some positive results. But eventually I grew discouraged. Although God was doing good things in our church, we didn't see as many conversions and baptisms as I'd hoped.

At this same time a sister church in our city was leading our convention in baptisms. I knew I was working as hard as that pastor, yet I wasn't seeing similar results. My father always taught me that as a pastor, I should take my faith to the people and my problems to God. That's what I did.

In a private prayer time in my office one morning, I poured out all the questions that had been troubling me. "Lord, don't You care about *our* community? Don't You love *my* church? Lord, I'm working as hard as I can. Why aren't You doing more in this church?"

The problem with asking God a hard question is that He may give you a hard answer. God spoke to me in a painfully clear way. In a nutshell He said, *Richard, I'm giving you all the success your character can handle. You have pride in your life, and if I were to bless your ministry like I'm blessing your colleague's, it would swell your ego to a place where I could no longer use you. You would become boastful and want to inform all your fellow pastors how God was blessing your ministry. Right now I'm more concerned about your walk with Me than about helping you succeed.*

That answer devastated me. I knew God was right. It shattered me to realize that the primary reason God wasn't blessing my church more was because of my pride. No one was working harder to grow the church than I was, yet my lack of personal growth had been stifling what God wanted to do.

> *I'd always been just one desperate, humble prayer away from God doing a fresh, new work through me.*

At that moment in my life and ministry I had to make a pivotal decision. I was still in my twenties. I realized if something didn't change in me, I was in danger of spending the remainder of my ministry wallowing in mediocrity. I couldn't bear the thought of wasting the next four decades of my life merely going through the motions. I earnestly pleaded, "Lord, whatever You have to do, please do it in me now." Of course, with that kind of prayer, you have to be ready for anything.

It wouldn't be so bad if God built character by showering you with blessings. But humility generally comes through hardship, criticism, and unfair treatment. The next year was filled with all that and more. I received letters filled with critiques of my performance. (Most pastors are familiar with anonymous letters attacking them; my appraisals were usually signed. I guess my antagonists wanted credit for their insights into my job performance.) Church members opposed me and questioned my motives. People left the church expressing anger toward me.

Whenever I was attacked, my sensitive ego would rise to my defense and prepare a thorough rebuttal to my critics. But the Holy Spirit would gently remind me how I'd invited Him to do whatever He had to do in my life—and He was doing it. Dealing with my pride wasn't easy.

Throughout that year I was so busy trying to survive attacks and barbs that I hardly noticed something: the church was growing. God was gradually but definitely blessing us. By year's end we'd enjoyed tremendous growth and were second in our national convention in the number of baptisms. (And although by that point I realized it was prideful to keep track of such things, I did inadvertently notice that our giving was way up too.)

It dawned on me that I'd always been just one desperate, humble prayer away from God doing a fresh, new work through me. As long as I was satisfied making excuses and blaming others for my lack of success, I stayed right where I was. As long as I focused on God changing my church members or my denominational leaders or the government or the economy, my ministry continued to muddle along. But the moment I cried out to God and pleaded with Him to work in *my* life, everything began to change.

I've come to understand that although God is the One who ultimately brings about change in me, I'm the one who must want it and ask Him to do it. If I don't, I'll limit what God does in my life.

THE CHALLENGE

Have you stopped growing? Have you spiritually unpacked your bags and permanently settled in where you are?

If you have, you need to get alone with God, as Jesus did, and ask Him what's on His heart for you.

You may be right on the brink of an entirely new dimension in your life. God may want to build something new on everything you've previously done. All your hardships and disappointments may be merely foundational to the mighty work God does next. You could be on the verge of experiencing the best days of your life.

Are you ready?

QUESTIONS FOR REFLECTION

1. List some things you know God has asked you to do. Include the small things. As you review the list, ask yourself this question: have I been faithful in a little?

2. Is there any area of your life where you've overestimated your ability to serve God? If so, what is it?

3. How is God presently growing you so you have a greater capacity to serve Him in the future? How have you been responding to God's activity in your life?

4. What evidence do you see that you've stopped growing spiritually, professionally, and personally?

5. How might you adjust your life so you continue to grow and accept fresh challenges?

FOUR

UNLIMITING
WHAT WE KNOW OF GOD

Ten days after our wedding, Lisa and I were blissfully on our way to seminary in Texas. Although we were newlyweds, we'd dated for two years before marrying, and I thought I knew Lisa quite well.

I was wrong.

OUT OF TOUCH AT A SPAGHETTI DINNER

Upon arriving at seminary we began meeting numerous young couples like ourselves who also had recently married. Everyone was trying to make new friends. In our first month there we received invitations to six different couples' homes. Every one of them served us spaghetti on their brand-new wedding china.

I remember one particular couple who were both extremely shy. When we arrived, the wife was in the kitchen frantically trying to salvage a pot of spaghetti noodles that had fused into a solid blob. The husband awkwardly tried to entertain us in their Spartan living room.

This young man was very nice, but stimulating conversation was not his forte. He was prone to one-word answers. Finally Lisa asked him what classes he was taking in school. He mentioned he was taking Old

Testament Survey. Immediately Lisa enthusiastically told him how interested she was in learning about the Old Testament and began peppering him with questions. He timidly began to answer and talk about what he was learning.

Quite frankly I was delighted with what I was hearing. I had no idea my wife was so fascinated with the first thirty-nine books of the Bible. As luck would have it, I was also taking Old Testament Survey but with a different professor. When our new friend began to falter in explaining to Lisa the various theories of creation and the authorship of Genesis, I jumped in with gusto, meticulously explaining the divergent scholarly theories, which one I favored, and why.

> *I never noticed the looks my wife was giving me.*

Each time I spoke, Lisa would quickly ask our friend another question. Eager to participate in the conversation, I would soon interject again and expound upon what our host said, filling in any important details he missed. I never noticed the looks my wife was giving me (if glares could kill!).

Finally our host was summoned into the kitchen where his wife was desperately trying to eradicate the pronounced scorched taste from the meat sauce.

"Why do you keep doing that?" Lisa whispered.

"Doing what?" I asked in surprise.

"Talking!"

The lights came on. She'd finally found a subject our host would talk about, but I'd mistakenly assumed she was actually interested in what we were studying at school. (She wasn't.) She'd been sending me all kinds of nonverbal cues; she'd done everything but shoot off emergency flares trying to send me a message, but I'd missed it.

Though Lisa and I were married, we didn't know each other very well. I misunderstood her methods of communication, so I completely missed the important message she kept sending. We shared life's most intimate relationship, but we were not yet in tune with one another. Fortunately for me, I grew quite familiar with "the look," which has served me well over the last twenty-four years.

Likewise, it's possible to enter a personal relationship with Jesus Christ and yet be largely unfamiliar with Him. When we become Christians, Christ invites us to get to know and experience Him at the deepest levels. Yet often we remain at a surface relationship with only a superficial knowledge of Him.

DEPTH, NOT LENGTH

The questions we ask God reveal a great deal about what's in our heart and mind, and some queries we wish we could take back. This was apparently even true of Jesus's twelve disciples.

In John 14, Jesus was talking with eleven of His disciples in the upper room after He'd shared the Last Supper with them, preparing them for His imminent departure. He told them, "I am the way, the truth, and the life. No one comes to the Father except through Me. If you had known Me, you would have known My Father also; and from now on you know Him and have seen Him" (14:6–7).

Philip jumped in: "Lord, show us the Father, and it is sufficient for us" (verse 8).

Jesus's response was humbling: "Have I been with you so long, and yet you have not known Me, Philip?" (verse 9).

Early in His ministry, Jesus had called Philip to follow Him (John 1:43–44). Philip had witnessed Jesus perform many miracles. He'd listened to Jesus preach and teach on numerous occasions. He'd visited with Jesus over dinner and while walking along the roadside. Few people had enjoyed the close proximity to Jesus that Philip had. Yet his request clearly revealed that despite all Jesus had done to teach His disciples who He was, Philip still had only a surface knowledge of his Lord.

Like Philip, Christians today can follow Jesus for years and yet have only a superficial knowledge of Him. It's possible to witness all manner of answers to prayer, expressions of God's love, and directions from God's Word, yet remain out of sync with Him.

It isn't the length of our relationship with Christ that matters, but its depth. Jesus taught His disciples this:

Christ will disclose to us only as much of Himself as we have the capacity to receive.

God invites each of us to spend time with Him and to get to know Him. But He doesn't force Himself upon us. Notice God's response at being rejected by His people: "And I spoke to you, rising up early and speaking, *but you did not hear,* and I called you, *but you did not answer*" (Jeremiah 7:13). Although He longed to meet with His people, they apparently did not care to spend time with Him.

Likewise His Word promises, "Draw near to God and He will draw near to you" (James 4:8). God's invitation stands: we're welcome to draw as near to Him as we desire. God sets no limit to how closely we can come to know Him. He doesn't restrict us to learning doctrines about Him or to voicing formal, rigid prayers to Him. His invitation is open ended. The limit to how close we draw to God lies with us. How close do we want to be?

Christian history holds inspiring accounts of men and women who took God's invitation extremely seriously and who spent their lives diligently pursuing God. Others observed the religious duties of attending church and living moral lives, but they never sought to really know God. They were content with status-quo spirituality, not bothering to seek a deeper relationship with their Father and Creator.

God is infinite. His character is so multifaceted that even if we were to spend every day for the rest of eternity trying to understand and know Him, we would not have plumbed the depths of His nature.

Think, for instance, of God's immeasurable love. How much love did it take for the almighty Creator to humble Himself to become a man so He could suffer on a cross and redeem His rebellious creatures from their sin? How much love does it take for God to know and deeply care about each individual among the billions of people inhabiting the earth? How long would it take us to fully comprehend the magnitude of God's love?

Or consider God's power. How much power did God need to create a universe out of nothing? to initiate human life? to defeat sin? to raise Jesus from the dead? How long would it take us to know the extent of God's power?

Think of God's wisdom. He knew how to create a universe. He's familiar with each cell that makes up the body of every person on earth. He witnessed every event in history, and He's completely aware of each situation that will occur in the future. There are no mysteries for God. He knows everything. How long would it take you to know the mind of God? He's willing to share it with you, but how long would it take Him to explain it to you? How long would it take you to understand an infinite God?

SEEKING GOD AT FOUR A.M.

It's been my privilege to write a number of books with my father. He's a tremendously busy man, so my greatest challenge is usually sitting him down long enough to capture his thoughts. Several years ago he was passing through my town, and we agreed to take a day to work on our latest book. Wanting to get the most out of that day, I informed him I would have the coffee ready at six a.m., and I expected him to be ready to put profound thoughts on paper. He looked at me with feigned disappointment and declared, "The world is going to hell in a handbasket, and my son is sleeping in until six a.m.!" (My dad rises at four every morning.)

The next morning at six I came down to the kitchen where we were going to work and found my dad already seated at the kitchen table. He had a stack of handwritten notes in front of him. As I poured my coffee and wiped the sleep from my eyes, he said, "Richard, let me read you something I found this morning." He began to read excitedly from Proverbs. He exclaimed, "These words are so true in describing what's happening in our world today!"

Then he told me how he'd cross-referenced these truths in Proverbs with a passage in Isaiah. As he shared what God had revealed to him that morning, he kept flipping through pages of the notes he'd taken.

> *"God is showing me there's still so much He wants to do in my life."*

Then he told me how God had led him to some passages in Jeremiah. Then he'd compared those Old Testament passages with what Jesus taught in the Gospels.

By the time Dad was finished showing me the message God had given him that morning, he'd reviewed twelve pages of notes. It was a little after six a.m. Dad looked up at me, and with tears in his eyes, he said, "God is showing me there's still so much He wants to do in my life."

That was a sacred moment for me. There in my kitchen the Holy Spirit whispered, *You can have the same deep walk with God your father has. You just have to be willing to seek after Me the way he does.*

My dad was in his sixties. He'd read his Bible for decades. Yet he was still getting up at four a.m. eager to discover what God had to say to him each morning. I came away from that experience asking myself, *How much do I really want to know God?*

WANTING MORE

The Scriptures testify about others who had an unusual desire to know God more deeply.

Moses was one of them. At Mount Sinai, the Israelites were terrified to encounter God's presence. After God declared that they were unprepared to draw any closer to Him, they stayed at the foot of the mountain, trembling in fear (Exodus 20:18–21). Moses,

> *Moses went far beyond his contemporaries in knowing God.*

on the other hand, wasn't content to remain so far away. He climbed up that intimidating mountaintop to meet with God.

Even that wasn't enough. Moses later asked God to show him His glory (Exodus 33:18–23). Almighty God responded in breathtaking splendor. Moses saw Him as no one had before.

Moses enjoyed such intimacy with God that whenever he came from God's presence, his face glowed (Exodus 34:29–35). When people saw his face, they knew he'd been close to the Lord. Moses went far beyond his contemporaries in knowing God.

The apostle Paul was another. He had been an exceedingly ambitious young man. Yet after meeting Christ, he was consumed with an entirely new passion: *knowing* Him.

Paul wrote,

> What things were gain to me, these I have counted loss for
> Christ. Yet indeed I also count all things loss for the excellence
> of the knowledge of Christ Jesus my Lord, for whom I have
> suffered the loss of all things, and count them as rubbish, that
> I may gain Christ and be found in Him, not having my own
> righteousness, which is from the law, but that which is through
> faith in Christ, the righteousness which is from God by faith;
> that I may know Him and the power of His resurrection, and
> the fellowship of His sufferings, being conformed to His death.
> (Philippians 3:7–10)

After he encountered the risen Jesus on the road to Damascus, Paul commenced his lifelong pursuit of knowing Christ. Paul was willing to sacrifice his reputation, his career, his health, even his life in order to know as much of Christ as he could.

As a result, Paul had experiences with God that few others did. He was even taken up into the third heaven and heard words spoken that he couldn't fathom or repeat (2 Corinthians 12:1–6).

Paul experienced God to a degree far beyond most Christians of his day. It wasn't that others were unable to know Christ at the same level as Paul, but that few others shared his fervent desire to do so.

Mountain Climbing

Each person who becomes a Christian is like someone who's invited to climb a majestic mountain. People respond differently to such a glorious opportunity. Some never leave the foot of the mountain. They gaze up at its grandeur and feel overwhelmed and inadequate to take on such a challenge. So they remain where they are.

Many others begin the journey up the slope. They find hidden meadows at the base of the mountain and ice-cold streams rushing down from the heights above. During this initial ascent, the slope is gradual, the path is wide and well traveled, and there are numerous signs of many others having passed this way before.

At the end of the day's journey, the weary climbers settle down to camp for the night. Sitting around campfires, they tell of their day's adventures. They recall the wildlife they encountered and the beautiful wildflowers they saw along *Others simply have grown content.* the path. It's a time of warm fellowship as various pilgrims relate their experiences and enjoy one another's company.

The next day the climbers prepare to push on to the next height. But not everyone is going. Some travelers complain of sore feet and decide to rest for a time before setting out on the trail again. Some have made new friends along the way, and they choose to linger behind so they have more time to enjoy fellowship with their new comrades. Others simply have grown content for now with the tranquillity of the campsite and lack the motivation to discover anything more.

To those who keep going, the trail appears less traveled but is still clearly marked as it climbs toward the peak. The slope is steeper here and somewhat narrower. The views are more impressive than they were the first day, and some of the travelers express regret that those who stayed behind are missing these breathtaking new vistas. They hope it won't be long before the others resume their climb.

As the days pass, each morning finds fewer hikers setting out on the climb. The pathway continues to narrow and is difficult at times to follow. The incline grows steeper and requires greater effort. But always, as the path becomes more demanding, the scenery becomes even more spectacular.

It isn't hard to find reasons to turn back. There are plenty of aches and pains. Some of the travelers develop conflicts with fellow hikers. Others note despondently that the summit never seems to draw nearer.

But a handful of dedicated and determined hikers continues to move upward, each one at his or her own pace. As they reach greater heights and discover stunning new scenes of beauty, the climbers often cannot find words to express what they're experiencing. These resolute few now communicate at

> *What they're viewing now will probably never be witnessed by those left behind.*

an unspoken level. They've each been through so much, and seen such spectacular sights, that they've become kindred spirits. Each knows the enormous effort the others have made to reach that height on the mountain. Each has been tempted to stop or to return, but all have overcome such enticements and pressed forward, often through great pain.

They seldom mention their former companions anymore. Everyone understands that what they're viewing now will probably never be witnessed by those left behind.

Eventually the trail disappears on the rugged slopes. It appears that hardly anyone has ever reached this height before. The climbers wonder about those very few who have come this far: Did they make it to the summit? Or were they overcome by fatigue or adversity before reaching their goal?

Finally, exhausted and spent, they slowly make their way up the steepest grade yet. The only thing pushing them upward is the thrilling realization that at last they're on the final ascent. Painfully but gratefully they reach the breathtakingly beautiful crest—only to discover it isn't the summit after all. Ahead of them rise higher slopes crowned majestically in clouds.

They keep going. Sometimes the highest peak appears beyond reach, but at other moments it seems attainable with one more day's effort. So those determined few press on.

Knowing the Lord is like climbing that mountain. The ascent is available to all, but not everyone reaches the same level. Each of us decides how much effort to expend to reach the heights; each of us ultimately decides how far and how high we'll go.

PRAYING HYDE

John Hyde, a missionary to India, had a deep desire to know Christ. He would spend extensive times in prayer, entering into such deep intercession that he would forgo food, sleep, and physical comfort.

On one occasion, during a missionary gathering, Hyde shared a room with several others, and one of them left this account of him:

> But one morning…he rushed in and went down on his knees
> by the bedside. This was in the early morning soon after dawn.
> I went to the *chota-hazri* (early breakfast) and came back and
> found him still praying. Then I went out to the prayer meeting
> and morning service, and came back about eleven o'clock, and

found him still praying.... At six o'clock he was still on his knees, and had been all day. As I had an hour to wait for dinner, I determined to watch him and if he arose from his knees, I would ask him how it was possible for him to remain the whole day and to pray while there was so much noise around, for people were coming and going the whole time.... In half an hour or so he looked up and smiled. I sat on his bed and asked what was the secret of all this.[3]

John Hyde's detailed answer began like this: "Let me tell you what a vision I had—a new vision of Christ."

The companion's account continues:

I shall never forget his words as they gave me a new vision of Christ.... I could not keep the tears back. At times I felt that it could not be true, that Christ had never suffered so much for me.... How I wish I could repeat it as Hyde brought me step by step to see Christ that evening.[4]

John Hyde—known as "Praying Hyde" for obvious reasons—was willing to pay any price, spend any amount of time, and exert any effort to know Christ more intimately and personally. As a result, he grew to know Christ in ways his contemporaries did not.

WHAT OUR PRAYERS REVEAL

Certain aspects of our Christian life reveal clearly whether we've developed a deep walk with God. One of these is our prayer life.

Have you ever prayed with someone whom you sensed was going places with God in prayer where you'd never been? It might have been a widow who had learned to depend on her Lord for her daily provision or someone who took great delight in communing with God and reaching the greatest heights of prayer.

Most Christians pray. For some, praying is merely the daily reciting of their prayer list to God. But other believers are dissatisfied with merely "saying" prayers. They want to enter sacred, elevated sanctuar-

> *Through our prayers, God transforms us.*

ies. For them, prayer means entering God's holy presence and communing with Him about His intentions and activity.

Prayer isn't merely for us to place our wishes before God; it's an opportunity for God to lay His heart upon us. When we've truly prayed, we come away with a heart and mind like God's. Through our prayers, we do not conform God to our will; rather He transforms us as we abide in His presence (2 Corinthians 3:16, 18).

As John Hyde understood, one does not reach the profoundest moments of prayer in a few minutes. We cannot rush in and out of God's presence and expect to have a deep, dramatic encounter with Him. We must ready our hearts to meet with the Lord (see Exodus 19:10–11; Joshua 3:5). We must be willing to remain still so we can hear all God has on His heart to say. The reason many of us do not hear God reveal more to us is that our time devoted to prayer is too rushed. If you want to discover the sacred, secret places of prayer, be prepared to spend sufficient time to journey there.

Throughout history, men and women like John Hyde have taken prayer to a higher level than the average Christian reaches. George

Müller, for example, provided for over ten thousand orphans in Bristol, England, solely through his powerful intercession. Müller would tell no one but God of his huge financial needs. Then daily he would watch as God moved in the hearts of His people to give to Müller's orphanage.

One reason so many Christians today do not experience greater dimensions of prayer is that they never hear this kind of praying from the pulpit. Most modern church services have "transitional prayers." Contemporary churches use prayer as a transition from one portion of the worship service to the next. The worship leader says a quick prayer (often a string of Christian clichés) while his worship team quickly and quietly moves onto the stage. Then he prays again while the pastor enters the baptistry. Then again while the worship team moves off the stage. All the prayers sound the same. Rarely are public prayers even a minute long.

This practice stands in stark contrast to church services of an earlier age. Charles Spurgeon was the famed pastor of London's Metropolitan Tabernacle. When visitors to the church were asked for their impressions of Spurgeon, they would readily acknowledge that his preaching lived up to its reputation, but they usually were most impressed by his prayers. People said it seemed as if Jesus was standing right next to Spurgeon when he prayed. When given the choice of preaching or praying in public services, Spurgeon chose to pray. He would bring the concerns, burdens, sins, and hurts of his people into God's presence. He would plead with God for deliverance and forgiveness for his dear people. Those who heard Spurgeon's intercession were convinced that he'd truly spoken with God and that God would respond.

Our generation is desperate for fervent, deep praying, but most Christians don't know how. Many pastors confess they spend insufficient time praying. A recent survey of churches identified fervent, faithful prayer as the number one need of the modern church. Intercession before God is imperative, yet too many Christians remain content with shallow platitudes.

OUR OBEDIENCE

Another way to measure how well you know God is to evaluate your obedience to His commands. In Christian circles, speaking of "wrestling" with God has become a fad. It sounds deceptively spiritual. People say they knew God wanted them to take on a volunteer position at their church, to go on a mission trip, or to change jobs, but they "wrestled" with Him about it for a long time before obeying. While I do not mean to minimize the difficulties people can face when they follow God, such "obedience" actually reflects procrastination and reluctance.

Almighty God sustains the universe. He gives life to every creature. He'll judge every person to determine his or her eternal destiny. Why would we argue with Him?

> *We misguidedly believe we can do something as ludicrous as grapple with our Creator!*

Or worse, why would we boast about doing so?

One day we'll be in heaven, standing before God's magnificent throne. Myriads upon myriads of angels will be shouting His praises, and all the saints will be lying prostrate before Him shouting, "Holy! Holy! Holy!" At that moment, numerous thoughts may pass through our minds, but "wrestling" with God will not be one of them! We will see God as He is, and we'll finally have a crystal-clear understanding of who we are in comparison.

Our problem in this life is that we don't know God well, so we misguidedly believe we can do something as ludicrous as grapple with our Creator!

We have no justifiable reason to wrestle with Him. "God is love" (1 John 4:8). Everything He does emanates from perfect love. Every word God speaks is characterized by pure, undefiled love. Why would we struggle against someone like that? Those who struggle to relate to perfect love simply do not understand God. When we become angry or bitter toward God, it reveals that we don't understand His heart and His compassion.

Jesus said, "He who does not love Me does not keep My words" (John 14:24). He made it clear: those who love Him obey Him. Out of an intimate walk with God flows spontaneous obedience. When we wrangle over doing what God says, that isn't an obedience problem but a love problem.

I know people who have come to love God so much that they obey Him as the angels do—instantly and without question. They trust Him totally. Even if something doesn't make sense to them, they don't second-guess Him. God spoke, so they gave their car to someone in need, sold their business, quit their lucrative job to work at a much lower salary for a Christian organization, forgave someone who hurt them deeply, enrolled in seminary, endured suffering, gave away their savings, or moved to another country.

As I travel, I hear countless testimonies from people who knew God was leading them to make a radical change in their life, and they didn't hesitate to obey because they were certain they could trust God completely with their life.

OUR CHRISTLIKENESS

Another reflection of how well you know Christ is the degree to which you're becoming like Him. When you spend a great amount of time with someone, you can't help being influenced by that person. You take on that individual's mannerisms and adopt his or her expressions.

My wife and I have experienced this. As I mentioned earlier, I used to be clueless when she was trying to send me discreet signals. But we've been married for twenty-four years. We've spent a lot of time together and have discussed life's issues in depth. I can mention a certain word now and she'll burst out laughing because that word represents a funny story. Or she can use a phrase that immediately reminds us of a special moment in our lives. We've shared so many experiences that I can anticipate what she'll think about certain situations.

Just before national elections one year, Lisa was too busy caring for our toddlers to follow the news. We were on our way one evening to a party where we knew political topics would likely be part of the conversation. Not wanting to appear ignorant in front of our new friends, she asked me, "Richard, what would my opinion be on the issues if I had time to have one?" We don't see eye to eye on everything, but we almost always know what the other one is thinking.

Likewise, as you spend time communing with Christ, you cannot help but take on His heart and mind. For instance, God is holy. He hates sin. You cannot spend day after day with a perfectly holy Being who hates sin and not grow to despise it too. Yet people who have been Christians for years tol-

People who have been Christians for years still live in continual fear and worry.

erate and even dismiss their sins, calling them "mistakes" or "poor judgment." Sin nailed Jesus to the cross—and the closer you are to Him, the more that reality will dramatically impact you.

God is also all-powerful. You cannot spend time with Him and not be encouraged and inspired (see Isaiah 40). Yet people who have been

Christians for years still live in continual fear and worry. If we truly know who God is, we'll realize we have no reason for anxiety.

God's nature is love (1 John 4:7–8). God acts in no other way but in a loving manner. As we spend time with Him, we cannot help but grow in loving others as well. It's impossible to refuse to act lovingly toward someone and still walk closely with the Lord.

Someone who has been a Christian for years but hasn't taken on the characteristics of Christ has not moved into a deep, intimate relationship with God.

RECOGNIZING GOD'S ACTIVITY

Those who know God intimately also recognize His activity around them.

The mighty prophet Elisha and his servant were being harassed by the Syrian army. During the night, enemy forces surrounded the city where Elisha was staying, intending to capture him and silence his prophecies (2 Kings 6:8–23). When Elisha's servant saw the menacing horde blocking their escape, he was greatly distressed.

Elisha was not. When the servant asked how Elisha could remain calm when he was about to be captured and executed, Elisha simply asked God to open his servant's spiritual eyes. Suddenly the terrified man perceived the presence of a mighty angelic host, ensuring that nothing would happen to God's servants.

Why did Elisha have a spiritual awareness that his servant lacked? They had different levels of relationship with God. Elisha knew God better. He knew where to look to see God's activity. His servant had a shallower relationship with God, so he'd been oblivious to the great work God was about to do right in front of them.

One day when Jesus was speaking to His disciples and they failed to grasp His meaning, He rebuked them:

Do you not yet perceive nor understand? Is your heart still hardened? Having eyes, do you not see? And having ears, do you not hear? And do you not remember?...

How is it you do not understand? (Mark 8:17–18, 21)

The disciples had been with Jesus for some time, yet they hadn't come to know and understand Him as they should have. Obviously Jesus felt they should have known Him better by that time.

Why are some people in tune with what God is saying while others are not? Why do some people quickly recognize God's activity and others do not? It has to do with the depth of their walk with God.

SPIRITUAL PERCEPTION AT WORK

When I was growing up, our family entered a phase where all four of us boys were teenagers and eating like there was no tomorrow. My father was a poor mission pastor and couldn't afford to feed and clothe his five kids. My mother finally decided to get a job (one that paid). She'd stayed home raising her children and serving as a pastor's wife for over twenty years. The only employment she could find was working as a nurse's aide at a nursing home.

The care facility housed some of the most miserable and hopeless people imaginable, such as victims of severe strokes and teenagers who had been paralyzed in motorcycle accidents. The residents knew they would spend the remainder of their lives lying in a bed, unable to care for themselves. Many of these people had been abandoned by friends, some even by their families. It was a lonely, depressing existence.

My mother did the most menial tasks in the center. She provided basic care for the patients and assisted the nurses. My mom always had a great attitude about such things. She would sing hymns as she went from room to room working. You could hear her all the way down the hallway. She would also pray for each patient as she worked in his or her room.

> *Nurses hurried down the hallway*
> *to see what was happening.*
> *It was a miracle!*

One long-term resident was a retired Methodist minister. A stroke had robbed him of the ability to speak. The medical team's numerous treatments and various medicines failed to restore his speech. The man's wife came faithfully to see him, but most of those to whom he'd ministered over the years had long since lost track of him. He was a helpless old man waiting impatiently to die.

One day Mom was working in his room, singing a great hymn of the faith, when she thought she heard a noise. Seeing no one there but the patient, she renewed her work and her singing. She heard the noise again. This time she saw something that made her catch her breath. The man's mouth was moving! It dawned on her that this man was trying to sing with her. She came close to his bed and resumed singing. His voice became stronger. Nurses hurried down the hallway to see what was happening. It was a miracle!

I believe almighty God looked out from heaven and had compassion on this weary, lonely saint. God chose to send him a message of hope to remind him that his Lord still remembered and loved him. And God used my mom to deliver the message.

In the following days my mother sang her entire inventory of hymns, and the man enthusiastically sang along. Then she began quoting half a Scripture verse, and he could complete it. They developed a special bond as together the two of them turned their eyes toward God.

That was a timely experience for my mother as well. In the midst of the mundane experiences of caring for hopeless, bitter people, she suddenly recognized the activity of God in that desolate place. Others might have missed it, but my mother had spent much time with the Lord and she recognized when He was at work. You don't have to have a PhD in theology or be fluent in New Testament Greek to recognize God working around you. You do have to spend time with Him so you know Him and recognize His activity.

RIDING THE ROLLER COASTER

When our children were young, Lisa and I would take them on an annual pilgrimage three hours north to the city of Edmonton. We sought refuge from the long, cold Canadian winter at the West Edmonton Mall, the largest mall in North America. This trip became a special family time each year in the midst of our frenetic schedules. The shopping oasis was filled with exciting things to do. Along with countless stores, it offered a large water park, an amusement park, an ice-skating rink, submarine rides (the mall claimed that it had more submarines than the Canadian navy), live dolphin shows, arcades, bowling lanes, miniature golf, movie theaters, food courts, simulation rides, and much more. All indoors!

One of our favorite areas was the enormous amusement park, which included rides for all ages. There was a children's area with a small train ride, a rope-ladder structure, and an area filled with plastic balls where kids could romp. At the far end of the massive play area stood a magnificent roller coaster. It did everything a roller coaster should do, including a heart-stopping drop at the beginning, three complete loops, and many other terrifying maneuvers. Because it was indoors, whenever the roller coaster plummeted down the tracks, the rattling noise would reverberate throughout the building. You could feel the vibrations.

As I would be playing with my kids in the plastic-colored-ball area, we would suddenly hear the roar of the roller coaster and the screams of passengers as it rattled mightily along the tracks. I would glance at the red colossus and wish my kids were old enough to go on it with me.

A walkway ran through one of the loops in the roller-coaster tracks, and each time we entered the amusement park, I would take my three kids and stand with them in the middle of that loop. We would watch as the roller coaster raced underneath us, then hurled itself upside down over our heads, and then whipped past. Each time the coaster soared by, I would look at my kids and say, "Doesn't that look like a lot of fun? Now *that's* a ride! Wouldn't you like to go with me on that?"

My children would always look at me dumbfounded and say, "Dad, you're crazy. We could be *killed* riding that! No way will we *ever* go on that."

Each time I assured them they would be perfectly safe. I promised to ride beside anyone who would go with me. I offered to hold their hand. I tried bribing them. I told them they could shut their eyes and I would tell them what was happening. Nothing worked.

Once they asked me why I didn't just ride the roller coaster by myself. "No, no, that won't work," I said. "It's no fun riding a roller coaster by yourself. It's only fun being terrified when you're with some-one you love!" (I should further explain that my wife is terribly afraid of heights and would rather die than ride a roller coaster—which seems paradoxical, since she's sure she would die if she rode one.)

Every year we made our family trip to that mall. Each time I would take my kids to that amusement park. There we would stand in the loop of that roller coaster. I would ask again if anyone felt ready to ride it with me. I always received the same response: "You're crazy!"

One year we visited my parents in Atlanta, and my mother went with us to Six Flags over Georgia. All day she endeavored to convince my children to try riding a roller coaster. She bribed them, flattered them, and promised them a pony, but with no success.

At the end of the day my mother, who loves roller coasters, had not ridden one. I agreed to go with her so she could have at least one good ride that day. Eagerly she walked off with me to ride the Ninja, an ominous-looking colossus.

I always received the same response: "You're crazy!"

Seeing her go, my youngest son's eyes bulged with fear. Clutching his mother's hand, in a quivering voice he pleaded, "Somebody's got to stop Grandma!"

As time went on, I grew desperate. My boys were plenty old enough to ride roller coasters, but they'd become so entrenched in their fear they couldn't bring themselves to try. So I did a devious thing. I invited a professor at our seminary to bring his family along with us to Edmonton. He had two boys around my sons' ages. I knew *they* would ride that roller coaster.

The evening before we were to go to the mall, my boys sheepishly approached me and informed me that, for the Blackaby name and honor, they would ride that roller coaster with me the next day.

The following morning my two boys and I joined the other family in line at the roller coaster. We were terrified—but the ride was fantastic.

It was exhilarating. My boys absolutely loved it. They insisted we purchase the exorbitantly priced photograph taken of us riding it so they could show all their friends. It had been the most exciting thing they'd ever done, and they had a profound sense of accomplishment. It was all they talked about.

The next year we went back to the mall. As we entered the amusement park, I began to head toward the area our kids always liked to go to first. "Dad, where are you going?" they asked. "The roller coaster is over there!" They'd lost all interest in the children's area once they'd experienced the roller coaster.

LOVING TO BE WITH HIM

Several years later, when my boys were sixteen and eighteen, I took them on a special father-son excursion. My son Mike cheers for the Colorado Avalanche hockey team (don't ask me why), while my son Daniel and I have rooted for the Buffalo Sabres for many years (I believe the reason is self-evident). We found the date when the two teams would play each other in Denver, cashed in some frequent-flier miles, and flew to Colorado.

> We've ridden the spiritual choo-choo train our entire Christian life, and we aren't sure we're ready for anything more challenging.

We spent the day at Elitch Gardens in Denver. This time my sons couldn't get enough of roller coasters. They dragged me all over the park. Of course, when you're a teenager these days, it isn't cool to be seen in public places with your ancient dad who's dressed like a tourist. But my boys didn't mind. All day they would point and shout, "Hey, let's do that one next! Oh, cool, look at that ride! Dad, hurry!" I got so tired I was practically begging to be left behind at the nearest cappuccino stand, but they would hear none of it.

At the close of the day we made our way out of the park toward the Pepsi Center, where my Sabres would gloriously triumph over the Avalanche. As we walked, my two teenage boys told me, "Dad, we've done a lot of fun things as a family before, but this has been the best thing we've ever done in our lives. We need to make this an annual event. Every year, even when we're old, fat, and married like you, we need to go to a different city and ride all their roller coasters and then see a hockey game." Of course you know what that did in my heart. Could there be any more precious words for a father to hear than that his children's favorite experience was spending time with him? We'd made some cherished memories together.

Through my experiences with my kids, I gained a glimpse of what God experiences as He relates to us. When we become Christians, we all begin as spiritual babies. We enjoy being in the spiritual children's area. It's all we can handle. But there's so much to experience of God. He's continually coming to us and inviting us to go deeper with Him in prayer, to reach new heights with His power, to go places with Him we've never dreamed of. But we're afraid. We've ridden the spiritual choo-choo train our entire Christian life, and we aren't sure we're ready for anything more challenging. But God patiently promises to go with us, to never leave us or forsake us, and to be right beside us through our next adventure with Him.

Unfortunately some Christians never move on. Despite the incredible invitation to know an infinite God, they remain in the spiritual playground and never know what could have been. At times they hear the sound of the roller coaster. They hear testimonies of those who have witnessed God's power in prayer. They listen to people excitedly share about new heights they reached with God. They read Christian biographies of those who came to know God in a powerful way, and they wonder what it would be like to reach those spiritual levels themselves. But they remain where they are.

Others step out in faith seeking to reach new spiritual heights. Just like my boys, once they reach a new level with God, they never want to go back. They're ruined for spiritual baby food once they've tasted spiritual meat. How it must please our heavenly Father when His children take Him by the hand and willingly go with Him wherever He leads them. How it glorifies Him when His children love to be with Him where He is.

The Challenge

I pray the Holy Spirit would create within your heart a holy restlessness. I hope you'll be discontent to remain where you are.

I want you to have a compelling desire, as the apostle Paul did, to know Christ in all His fullness. May you never be content to merely hear how others have grown to know the Lord more deeply, but may you strive for that experience too.

God has invited you to know Him. Don't stay where you are. Ask Him to guide you to a new spiritual level, starting today.

Questions for Reflection

1. What new truths have you learned about Christ recently?
2. What new spiritual levels have you recently reached?

3. How does your life reflect that of someone who knows Christ intimately? What about your prayer life? your Christlikeness? your obedience?

4. What evidence is there that you're becoming holy as God is holy? For example, do you have a heart for forgiveness as God does?

5. What are you presently recognizing about God's activity around you?

FIVE

UNLIMITING GOD'S POWER
IN OUR LIVES

As a child I spent a lot of time playing with my brother Tom, who's thirteen months younger than I. Being a pastor's kids, our favorite game was "church." I would be the preacher, and Tom was always the worship leader. (He said in heaven they won't have preachers anymore, but they'll always need worship leaders!) Together we would conduct moving and heartfelt worship services from the top of our bunk bed. We had space in our bedroom to set only one chair in the middle of the floor, so we'd always invite our mother to be the congregation. (We knew she needed a lot of church.)

The service would commence with Tom making the obligatory announcements. "Today we'll have an ice-cream potluck social immediately after the service. We hope you'll all bring *lots* of ice cream!" Then Tom would lead us in singing all the songs we knew. My mother would enthusiastically participate. When we exhausted our musical repertoire, Tom would announce, "And now our pastor is going to come and deliver God's Word to us."

I would open my children's Bible and expound on God's Word. I'd developed some rudimentary sermon notes from which I preached. I had only one sermon, but I always delivered it with passion, conviction, and a profound sense of urgency. It was titled "The Sin of Spanking Your Children." As I warmed to my theme, I would proclaim: "There may be some here today who have committed this sin against your own flesh and blood and against almighty God. Even now the Spirit of God is urging you to turn back from your wicked and evil ways."

I usually felt led to extend an altar call so people in the congregation could immediately get right with the Lord. When no one came forward, I would stop the music and state, "Now, folks, we're not in any hurry. We'll continue to sing until *everyone* has had a chance to be made right with God!"

Eventually, to mercifully bring closure to the ordeal, my mother would "walk the aisle" and rededicate herself to becoming a better mother. We would close the service and hurry to have ice cream.

Unfortunately it never took long for our mother to backslide (on our backsides!), and we would be compelled to hold another meeting. After one particularly unpleasant week of discipline, Tom complained to me in frustration, "These church services aren't changing Mom. I think she needs a whole revival meeting!"

We obviously had much to learn about ministry at that formative stage of our lives, but we did discover one thing. Just going through the motions of conducting a service and preaching a sermon didn't mean anyone's life was being changed. We also realized that even though we *wanted* God to use us mightily, that didn't guarantee He would do so. That was His prerogative.

Whether we like it or not, there are limits to how much of God's power we will experience in our lives.

Too Difficult for God?

The Gospels record a troubling moment when Jesus's disciples reached the limit of God's power in their lives. Their public ministry had begun well, as Jesus gave them power and authority to cast out evil spirits (Mark 6:7). There's much debate about what such power involves. I like to view God's power as His means of setting people free. God's power can liberate people from illness, demon possession, fear, pride, anger, or any bondage sin brings. When Jesus sent His disciples out by twos throughout the countryside, it was to set people free.

Their mission was extremely successful. They cast out many demons and healed numerous sick people (Mark 6:13). They preached the gospel and saw many repent of their sin.

But later, while Jesus was away with Peter, James, and John on the Mount of Transfiguration, a desperate father brought his only son to the other nine disciples. This boy's problem proved more than they could handle. Jesus's disciples had clearly been given the power to cast out unclean spirits. They had done it many times before. But on this occasion, all nine of these disciples were stymied.

When Jesus rejoined them, "He saw a great multitude around them, and scribes disputing with them" (Mark 9:14). The scribes were probably ridiculing the disciples, having a field day mocking them for their public failure. The disciples had claimed God's power in their lives, but it wasn't evident that day.

When Jesus asked what was going on, the scribes didn't answer, and the humiliated disciples said nothing. But the desperate father spoke up. "Teacher," he said, "I brought You my son, who has a mute spirit. And wherever it seizes him, it throws him down; he foams at the mouth, gnashes his teeth, and becomes rigid" (verses 17–18). Sorrowfully he related how he'd begged Jesus's disciples to set his only child free, *"but they could not"* (verse 18).

Then came Jesus's startling rebuke: "O faithless generation, how long shall I be with you? How long shall I bear with you?" (verse 19).

His reprimand was directed at *faithlessness.* Jesus promptly set the enslaved boy free.

Later, in private, the chagrined disciples asked Jesus why they'd been so helpless. Jesus's response: "This kind can come out by nothing but prayer and fasting" (verse 29). Jesus was declaring that this particular situation was indeed difficult, but not impossible.

> *The first place God points to when we face difficulties is our prayer life.*

Frankly, I'm grateful for Jesus's acknowledgment that some situations are more challenging than others. Some people espouse the belief that everything in the Christian life is easy if you have sufficient faith. Yet Jesus recognized that some kinds of bondage can be overcome only through prayer and fasting.

This event revealed what the disciples had *not* been doing. The first place God points to when we face difficulties is our prayer life.

I've spoken with pastors who were about to be fired from their troubled churches. When I asked about their prayer lives, they sighed and confessed that with all they'd been going through lately, they had scant time to pray. Churches that fall into disunity and conflict inevitably have far more people attending the business meetings than the prayer meetings. Couples whose marriages are disintegrating will often spend more time with counselors or lawyers than in prayer.

Jesus would point us to the same place He directed His disciples: prayer. If you come across a difficult situation, start praying.

Jesus also recommended fasting. Fasting involves setting aside normal routines and focusing on God and His answer for your situation. It entails sacrifice. It means that business as usual is insufficient for the situation.

The disciples' problem was that they believed they'd encountered a problem too difficult even for God's power. They'd given up. When

Jesus appeared on the scene, His disciples could have immediately rushed up and said, "Master, we're working on a really difficult case, and we need Your help. We know God's power can set this boy free, but this situation is pretty bad. The father is distraught. The boy is in terrible bondage. We promised that when You came, You would set him free." In reality, the disciples said nothing. They'd already given up.

There's no situation more hopeless than when God's people give up on someone.

The disciples were undoubtedly embarrassed at their failure. Rather than persevering in their efforts to free the boy, they became embroiled in an argument with the scribes as they defended their tarnished reputations.

Their failure to heal the boy implied that some cases were too difficult even for God. Put another way, the disciples believed there was a limit to what God's power could do. They knew God could set *some* people free, because they'd experienced it. But in their limited spiritual maturity, this boy's problem seemed beyond the scope even of God's power.

I can imagine their thoughts and conversations after their failure: "Wow! Satan really has a stronghold in that boy's life! You just can't help people who don't want to be helped." With those unimpressed scribes who were looking on, they might have debated various theories on why the boy remained in bondage. Meanwhile the boy continued to convulse on the ground.

HELP MY UNBELIEF!

By contrast, look closely at how Jesus responded when the boy was brought to Him and began to wallow on the ground and foam at the mouth.

He asked [the boy's] father, "How long has this been happening to him?"

And he said, "From childhood. And often he has thrown him both into the fire and into the water to destroy him. But if You can do anything, have compassion on us and help us."

Jesus said to him, "If you can believe, all things are possible to him who believes."

Immediately the father of the child cried out and said with tears, "Lord, I believe; help my unbelief!"

When Jesus saw that the people came running together, He rebuked the unclean spirit, saying to it, "Deaf and dumb spirit, I command you, come out of him and enter him no more!" Then the spirit cried out, convulsed him greatly, and came out of him. And he became as one dead, so that many said, "He is dead." But Jesus took him by the hand and lifted him up, and he arose. (9:21–27)

The boy's father had desperately sought his son's deliverance for years. No one had wanted the boy to be set free more than he did. Yet when he came to Jesus, he discovered that the problem had never been with God. Jesus pointed to the man's faith.

"If you can believe," Jesus told him, "all things are possible to him who believes" (verse 23). Didn't the father believe? After all, look at all he'd done to procure his son's healing.

The father did have *some* faith, but his faith hadn't been at a level to see God work miraculously in his son's life. There was a limit to the man's belief in what God could do. After all, he'd seen that even Jesus's own disciples failed to set the boy free.

When this man heard Jesus's response, he didn't offer any excuses. He didn't list all the doctors he'd taken his son to see. He didn't complain about the failure of Jesus's disciples. Instead he pleaded with Jesus to raise the level of his own faith to a place where God would be pleased to set his son free. For in a sense, the limit to the father's faith had been costing the son his freedom.

Could it be that the limits to your faith have been costing others around you? As a husband, father, and church member, I don't want my lack of belief in what God can do to prevent those I love from experiencing God's power and deliverance. That's why I regularly pray along the lines of what that boy's father prayed: *Lord, I do have a lot of faith in You already, but would You raise my faith in You to a higher level, so those I pray for and minister to can experience Your power in an even greater degree?*

I've met many dear Christian parents who have grieved over a wayward child. Husbands and wives have prayed for years for their unbelieving spouse's salvation. Church members have grieved over those

> *The limit to the father's faith had been costing the son his freedom.*

who've fallen into sin and left their fellowship. After years of futility, we easily can become like the disciples and assume there's nothing more that can be done.

In reality, Jesus might challenge us as He challenged the boy's father, to allow Him to raise our level of faith to a new level. When we accept limits to our faith, it costs others. Where in your life right now do you need God to raise your level of faith in Him?

The principle we can learn from this event in Mark 9 is this:

God gives to us according to our faith.

It's easy to believe God for generalities; it's much harder to trust Him for specifics. "I believe God is omnipotent" is a fine statement. "I believe God can heal this demon-possessed boy on the ground in front of me" takes far more faith. The disciples believed God in general, but they failed to trust Him for this specific situation.

Likewise it's easy to praise God for His power and love during a Sunday worship service; it's quite another thing to trust that power and love as we go to work on Monday.

Have you set a limit on what you believe God can do in your life? There are several ways to tell.

For example, have you given up on someone or on yourself? Perhaps there's an area of constant struggle and defeat in your life. Maybe your painful past keeps causing you heartache. You've prayed for God to free you from its grip, but you still find yourself in bondage to its memories. Or maybe a sinful habit or an ungodly attitude afflicts you. After years of struggle you've concluded you'll never gain victory in this area. If this is your experience, you're limiting what you allow God to do.

Perhaps you prayed regularly for a friend's salvation, but after witnessing and inviting him to church on numerous occasions without result, you gave up and began focusing on others who were more responsive. When you stop praying, you've stopped believing.

Or maybe your sister is living a destructive lifestyle. You've prayed for her and pleaded with her, but she persists in her sin. After years of frustration you've finally resigned yourself to the reality that she'll never change. When you give up like that, you're saying loud and clear, "I don't believe God's power is adequate to make a difference in this situation."

This is often what churches are inadvertently saying when they "clean the church rolls." Well-intentioned church leaders occasionally review the long list of names of church members who haven't attended a service in years. They conclude that they should remove those names from church membership so the records more accurately reflect who attends. The problem is that a long list of inactive members is a visible testimony that the church was unable to help these people. God's power was apparently insufficient for the church to set these members free from their bondage and sins. It seems easier to move on and put these failures behind them than to be continually reminded of these hurting people.

Another clue that you're limiting your access to God's power is fear or anxiety. The Bible says worry is clear evidence that you do not trust God to care for you in your particular situation. We are peculiar people; we can face some challenging circumstances and never bat an eye, then worry ourselves sick when a different situation comes along. Each of us has fetishes and fears that we suspect even God cannot overcome.

> *The problem is that we tend to think small.*

For many people, public speaking falls into this category. They would rather climb a mountain or drive a unicycle through rush-hour traffic than stand before their church and share what happened on a recent mission trip. For some people, the fear of having to confront someone who's sinning is paralyzing.

This may sound harsh, but bashful people suffer greatly from fear. While many people are fundamentally shy, the truth is that shyness can lead to a form of self-centeredness. When this happens, these individuals become overly concerned about what people think of them. What if something they say makes them look foolish? What if people laugh at them? What if they say the wrong thing? Will people think less of them? When a person's focus is on himself, he can remain oblivious to how God wants him to meet the needs of others.

My dad is by nature an introvert. Yet his shyness has caused him to be keenly aware of his dependence on God every time God leads him to speak in public. Either God is all-powerful or He isn't, and since the answer to that is obvious, we're the ones who ensure our own failures when we refuse to trust Him.

Much of God's kingdom work around the world has been left undone because the Christians whom God wanted to use for His purposes were too intimidated to speak up. When you fail to stand up for your Lord, you're saying that even God's power and wisdom cannot help you make a difference in someone's life.

God can do anything He chooses to do in us and through us. The problem is that we tend to think small (like the people of Nazareth in Matthew 13:58).

Where's the ceiling on *your* belief? What is it you're struggling to trust Him for? What situation in your life seems hopeless? Ask God to help your unbelief, as the father of the demon-possessed boy did, so you're in a position to experience powerful new dimensions of God's work in you.

A FIRST GLIMPSE OF GOD'S POWER

The Lord is never content to leave us where we are spiritually. He took His inexperienced disciples and continued to teach them until they became bold miracle-working apostles. He'll also work in us until we're prepared for Him to do greater and greater works through us.

We Christians are meant to keep growing in our understanding of God and in trusting His power in our lives. We should be continually growing in our experience of God's power—unless we accept limitations on what we think God can do through us.

God has been expanding my trust in Him throughout my life. He began working on my faith when I was young. I almost flunked kindergarten. I was so fearful of "big kids" at school that my teacher concluded I wasn't prepared to advance to first grade.

One day my worst fears were realized. When unexpected company arrived at our house, my mother forgot to pick me up at school. I had to walk home through a sea of intimidating big kids. As I nervously made my way along, two older boys began following me. They could plainly see I was fearful, and they couldn't resist teasing me.

Oranges that had fallen from fruit trees were lying in the street (this was in Southern California), and the two boys began kicking them so they bounced against the back of my feet. I was walking as quickly as I could ahead of them. I was too afraid to run, knowing they would catch me if I did.

Fearfully trudging along, I fervently prayed for God to deliver me. As soon as I prayed, I was immediately aware that something had changed. I glanced behind me, and to my astonishment the bullies had vanished. I looked into the yards nearby to see if they'd turned off into one of them, but they were gone without a trace. I don't know how they could have disappeared so quickly.

> They could plainly see I was fearful.

I still vividly remember that day. I stood on that sidewalk and wondered what my prayers had just done to those two boys! It was the first time I realized how powerful and trustworthy God is.

GOD AND A GANG

Years later, having recently graduated from university, I served as a summer missionary. Another fellow and I were doing an evangelistic door-to-door survey in an exceedingly unchurched neighborhood. As we worked our way down one street, we noticed a formidable-looking gang house at the corner. The glass from the windows had all been knocked out. The yard was a wasteland. The house resembled a fortress. We desperately hoped no one was home.

When we were only two houses from the corner, we heard an ominous rumbling noise that grew steadily louder. It was the roar of a large fleet of motorcycles approaching. Our hearts sank. Sure enough, an intimidating biker gang sped past us and pulled up on the desolate lawn of their clubhouse.

As the gang members dismounted and prepared to enter their base, my partner and I desperately prayed that the house before theirs would be inhabited by a lonely widow who had just baked a chocolate cake and

> *The rest of the gang circled around, prepared to carry out whatever their boss ordered them to do to us.*

would insist that we spend the next few hours visiting with her. No such luck. No one was home.

As we walked back to the sidewalk, we read each other's mind and silently concurred that the gang would probably not be responsive to our survey. They seemed quite busy, and we thought it might be rude to disturb them. We decided to call it a day and prepared to return home.

"Hey, you guys, come here!" a gruff voice beckoned. To our dismay, it was a leather-clad behemoth, still mounted on his Harley. We meekly obeyed.

"What are you doing around here?" he growled.

The rest of the gang circled around, prepared to carry out whatever dastardly deed their boss ordered them to do to us. We timidly explained that we were starting a church and were surveying the neighborhood to find people who were interested in learning more about God.

We waited for the hammer to fall. To our relief, a broad grin swept across his face. He told us he believed in God too. He recounted how just the week before he'd been riding his motorcycle on a busy street when a car had cut him off in traffic. He was so furious he sped up beside the errant vehicle and made an obscene gesture at its driver. Then he noticed that the driver was wearing a clerical collar. It was a man of the cloth! Moments later, the biker rear-ended another vehicle and was almost killed.

"God got me for that," he explained. "I believe in God," he declared matter-of-factly. "I'm afraid of Him."

To my enormous relief, I'd been reminded again of God's power.

Meeting God

God also taught me much about His power when I became a pastor. Earlier I mentioned that my church had suffered steady decline for several years. Only a small group was left. Then summer came. People who know I live in Canada often ask me, "I know the winters in Canada are long and cold, but what do you do there during the summer?" My reply: "Well, if it happens to fall on a Saturday, we have a picnic!" Summertime is so precious to Canadians that people head to the lake and to campsites in droves. Our small church suddenly got a lot smaller.

Then, at the lowest summer ebb of our church attendance, a new family visited our church. They'd moved to our city a few months before and were looking for a church home. The father was a well-to-do businessman whose family was accustomed to the best. They had four children and had been attending one of the largest, most popular churches in the city. It boasted a beautiful new facility with cutting-edge technology and extensive children's programming, all of which our little church lacked. But on that particular morning, they'd decided on the spur of the moment to visit our church.

Quite frankly, it was embarrassing. Our regular worship leader was away on vacation, as were our second- and third-string backups. Our regular piano player was gone too. Needless to say, the music was awful. (On those Sundays, I used to tell my wife on the way home, "After being

> I thought I would salvage
> what dignity I could.

exposed to music like that, I feel a desperate need to go home and take a shower.") As the music continued that morning, I was sure our first-time visitors would never darken our church doorway again (if they even remained until the end of the service).

When it came time for the announcements, I thought I would salvage what dignity I could. I welcomed the few who had come and repeatedly mentioned how we had a *lot* of people out of town that morning. Then I casually mentioned how our *regular,* talented worship leader (who could sing) was on vacation that week. I expressed gratitude to the poor deacon who had been pressed upon to lead the music for us that morning. I also thanked the *substitute* piano player who had been willing to brush off the dust from her prehistoric piano book to fill in so cheerfully. I subtly put in that our normal accompanist was away that Sunday (probably doing a European concert tour).

As I sat down and the service continued, I felt uneasy. The Holy Spirit convicted me that I was embarrassed to be ministering in such an inauspicious setting that day in front of visitors. I felt self-consciously that our modest church had nothing to offer these sophisticated guests. The Spirit whispered to my soul: *Don't ever be embarrassed about representing your Lord. If you speak for Him in front of thousands of people or you talk about Him to a prisoner in a jail cell, it is an undeserved honor.* He reminded me that I had almighty God's power at my disposal whether I had a two-hundred-voice choir backing me up or was leading a small Bible study in an apartment building.

I felt convicted for my pride and self-centeredness. I also realized I'd spent all my time before the congregation that morning pointing out what was *not* at the church. In reality, the problems and inadequacies were painfully apparent to everyone. What they desperately needed to have brought to their attention was what was right. I should have been pointing people to God. He was there that morning, prepared to change lives and to set people free—but the people needed to be reminded of it.

I preached that morning like I never had before to that tiny group in that sweltering auditorium.

To my great surprise, the visiting family showed up again the following Sunday. I was so shocked that instead of welcoming them as they entered the building, I asked why they returned. The man explained that a lot of our people appeared to be away from our church last Sunday, so they thought they'd try it again. (It wasn't any better a week later.)

Each Sunday that summer I was sure this family would never return, and each Sunday they came back.

At the close of a service several weeks later, they came forward during an altar call to announce they wanted to become members of our church. I was so surprised, I asked them to address the congregation.

At first it was awkward. The man explained how initially they'd been attending a large church that had great kids' programs, first-class music, and ultramodern facilities. The man confessed that they decided each Sunday morning to return to that megachurch, reasoning that it could better meet their needs—but then they somehow ended up in our parking lot.

That morning, when it happened again, he had turned to his wife and asked, "Why do we keep coming back here when it has so much less to offer us than the bigger church?"

His wife responded, "Because every time we come here, we meet God."

And *that's* what people are looking for. We had just as much of God to offer people as the largest church in the city. People could have their lives transformed just as dramatically in our little auditorium as in the greatest cathedral. While I served as pastor of that church, I learned that the power of God could take the most humble church setting and do anything He purposed to do. There are no limits with God.

Over the following years, God repeatedly taught me that His presence and power in my life were sufficient to accomplish whatever He intended. When I later served as a seminary president for thir-

> *"Every time we come here, we meet God."*

teen years, we often faced a seemingly insurmountable deficit or an impossible situation—yet every time God proved that trusting in Him was never in vain. God kept putting me in situations where the potential was great, but where I would fail unless He intervened. Through these experiences, God took me deeper in my trust in Him. With each test, I experienced His power to a greater degree. There was always more He wanted to do in my life, but He first sought to increase my capacity to trust Him. Through those years God stretched my faith and helped me believe I could trust Him in every situation.

The limit to my experience of God's power rested not with God, but with me. His power is limitless; my faith is still growing.

MORE POTS

There's a wonderful story in the life of the prophet Elisha, in 2 Kings 4:1–7, that illustrates this principle.

> God invites each of us
> to prepare for what He intends
> to do in our lives.

Elisha was approached by a desperate, impoverished widow. Her creditor was coming to take away her two sons and sell them into slavery as compensation, and she was frantic to save her children.

Elisha asked what she possessed. All she had of value was one jar of oil.

He instructed her to gather all the containers she could borrow from her neighbors. "Do not gather just a few," he urged her. She was to pour her meager amount of oil into those containers, then "set aside the full ones."

If God gave *you* that message, how many containers would you collect? When would you decide you had gathered enough?

The prophet knew that the only limit to what God would do was how aggressively the woman believed and obeyed.

The woman and her sons gathered pots and took them inside their house. At a certain point they decided they'd amassed enough. She began pouring oil from her original container into the borrowed ones. The oil miraculously kept flowing until she had filled the last pot.

Seeing this miraculous supply, the widow called out to her son, "Bring me another vessel." But they'd used all the containers they had. "So the oil ceased."

Then Elisha instructed her to sell the oil, pay off her creditors, and live on the rest.

The flow of oil ceased because the widow had no capacity to receive anything more from God. It wasn't that God couldn't keep the oil coming; the woman simply was incapable of receiving any more. Had she collected containers more aggressively, she would have received more oil and earned more money.

As it was, God responded to the level of her faith. Did the woman sin in not gathering more pots? No. She received according to her faith.

Likewise God invites each of us to prepare for what He intends to do in our lives. Some people expect God to do great and mighty things, so they organize themselves accordingly. Others have smaller expectations, and as a result they aren't disappointed.

What God wants to do in each of our lives is to expand our trust in Him so we gather an enormous number of pots—because we believe God will do a fantastic work.

We Set the Limit

When Jesus came to His hometown of Nazareth, people had low expectations for this carpenter's son. As a result, "He did not do many mighty works there because of their unbelief " (Matthew 13:58). Could Jesus have performed more miracles? Certainly. But the people did not believe He could, so He didn't.

Matthew 14:25–32 relates a vivid account of someone who reached the limit of what he believed God could do. After Jesus fed the five thousand, His disciples boarded a fishing boat and made their way across the Sea of Galilee. A strong

> *To Peter's credit, he got out of the boat and began to walk on the water.*

wind suddenly arose, causing the waves to beat violently against the craft. To the disciples' amazement, Jesus arrived, walking on the water. "Be of good cheer!" He told them. "It is I; do not be afraid."

Peter spoke up (as usual): "Lord, if it is You, command me to come to You on the water." That was impressive. The other disciples didn't offer to leave the safety of the boat. Peter had great faith and believed he could do the impossible when Jesus was with him.

Jesus responded, "Come."

To Peter's credit, he got out of the boat and began to walk on the water (the only other person besides Jesus ever to do so). Peter was experiencing a level of God's power he'd never known before. But then he took his eyes off his Master. He began to notice the waves, and doubts assailed him. God's power had enabled him to take a few steps on water, but he began to wonder if it could sustain him there. He'd surpassed the limit of his fellow disciples' faith—but he eventually reached the boundary of his own belief. Everyone has a limit.

LIMITED CHURCHES

Every local church has unlimited potential. Christ is its Head as well as its Builder (Colossians 1:18; Matthew 16:18–19). With these divine resources, churches ought to be turning the world upside down. But they aren't. The reason is that congregations also have limits to what they believe God will do through them.

Many churches assume God will never ask them to do anything that isn't covered in their budget, so they don't attempt ministries beyond that. Congregations that split, with both sides remaining alienated, are acting as if they don't believe God's mighty power is adequate to bring reconciliation with their brethren. Churches remaining stagnant or in decline reveal their belief that God cannot revive them. Pastors who leave their church in frustration after only one or two years indicate their lack of faith that God can use them to turn the church around. Churches who refuse to start mission churches because they don't want to sacrifice members are assuming God will not fill the void. You can tell far more about a congregation's beliefs by their actions than by reading their church constitution.

DIVINE WAITING

I'm aware of one church in South Africa that lost sight of God, and the church eventually divided over styles of church leadership and worship. The pastor took the majority of the members and departed to begin a new church. The small remnant left behind was devastated. With fewer than forty members left, they were unsure if they could afford to hire another minister. God eventually led a pastor named John to them.

Upon his arrival, John gathered his tiny congregation and asked them to consider what God wanted to do through them. The group pointed out that they were only a handful and they couldn't afford to maintain their facility, let alone pay a pastor. It seemed ludicrous to consider what great work God was going to do through them. Eventually someone mentioned the extensive squatters' camp of black Africans positioned near their church building. A large percentage of the people living in that ghetto were HIV-positive. Venereal disease was epidemic. Unemployment was widespread. Fires would rage through the quarters and devastate hundreds of homes. This massive segment of humanity was hurting and hopeless, yet the Caucasian church had never ministered to them.

The tiny church was dwarfed by the extensive settlement, but the congregation determined to see if God would use them to minister in some small way. They began some simple programs to care for the peoples' most pressing needs. Eventually these expanded until the church was conducting over seventy different ministries, including the distribution of AIDS medicines, an AIDS hospice, a food pantry, a clothing pantry, a furniture bank, a Christian radio station, skills training, nutrition training, childcare instruction, medical care, education, and numerous other programs. Not surprisingly, the building was filled with enthusiastic new members who found satisfaction and meaning from being part of a church that was making such a significant difference in their city.

> *They've experienced God's power firsthand.*

When the United States launched a massive campaign to combat AIDS in Africa, they made billions of dollars available to organizations that were already dealing with the problem. More than four hundred faith-based organizations in Africa applied for funding, but only two were initially approved. This church was one of them. The pastor flew to Washington DC to meet with top White House advisors.

My father and I met with the pastor in Africa two weeks after he returned. The American government committed to provide $450,000 annually to support the church's efforts against AIDS. The pastor was still in shock when we met with him. At one point it seemed as if this church was so insignificant no pastor wanted to work with it; now even the White House wanted to get involved! Today when you ask members there about the limits on their church, they'll confidently tell you there are none. They've experienced God's power firsthand.

Can you imagine the unlimited possibilities for churches all over the world if they truly believed that God, the Head of their church, is all-powerful?

In times such as ours, with so many needs and so many people looking for hope, it's unforgivable that churches would settle for less than all God intends to do through them.

THE CHALLENGE

We serve a God so powerful He created an entire universe out of nothing. He holds every star and galaxy in its place. He took a lump of clay and created a living human being. He gives life to every person on earth, and He'll hold every person accountable in judgment for his or her actions. He's an all-powerful God.

This same God seeks to walk with us through each day. He intends to use our lives for His divine purposes. The possibilities are infinite. There's *nothing* God cannot do.

Yet sadly, despite the fathomless potential for Christians to experience God's power, many continue to live in defeat and discouragement. The problem is never with God. God has proven throughout history that no human condition or situation exceeds His ability to do a miracle. The limiting factor is always us. We may acknowledge that God has done miracles in the past. We may affirm that He accomplishes powerful works in peoples' lives today. But do we believe God will perform miracles in *our* lives? The way we're living clearly reveals what we believe.

Perhaps you've been experiencing God working in your life in some areas, but in others you consistently suffer failure. The pressing questions for you are these: What area of your life is presently not tapping into God's power? In what circumstance do you doubt God will do a great work? Is there a situation in your life in which you need to cry out to your Lord, "I do believe; help my unbelief"?

QUESTIONS FOR REFLECTION

1. In what areas of your life do you struggle to believe God?
2. Would you say your life reflects a strong belief that God can do anything? What is the evidence?
3. What is your church experience like? Does your church act on the belief that God can do anything? As a church member, are you helping others to trust in God?
4. In what areas of your life does God want to increase your faith?

SIX

UNLIMITING GOD'S JOY
IN OUR LIVES

M y wife, Lisa, loves a party, and she'll seize any occasion to throw one.

When our kids were in elementary school, Lisa organized an end-of-school-year beach party. The fact that we lived a thousand miles from the beach did not deter her. She transformed our backyard into a tropical oasis with a wading pool, water slide, Beach Boys music, beach toys, beachballs, tropical drinks and fruits, and (best of all) water guns. Lisa bought a water gun for each child. Since Mike and Daniel were older, she found them each a turbo-powered, pump-action water cannon. These puppies were stronger than a fire hose. You could level small buildings with the force of their spray. For Carrie, our preschool princess, there was a water pistol small enough to fit into her delicate hands.

The water fight commenced and mayhem ensued. As older

> *No one was prepared for the devilish metamorphosis that followed.*

brothers do, my sons ambushed their unsuspecting sister. Huge streams of water drenched Carrie to the bone. She bravely fought back, her little weapon spurting meager dewdrops.

Lisa noticed what was happening and moved to rescue her beleaguered daughter. But before Lisa reached her, Carrie laid aside her defective pistol and reached for a far more lethal weapon: her feminine charm.

Suddenly my four-year-old daughter wielded her cutest grin, batted her little eyelashes, and with her well-trained baby voice entreated her brother, "Daniel, my gun isn't working. Could I try yours for minute?" Daniel, smitten by her charming ways, glanced at his mother and shrugged as if to say, "How can I resist such cuteness?" He good-naturedly handed over his weapon.

No one was prepared for the devilish metamorphosis that followed. Carrie's lips curled into a menacing sneer. Her sparkling eyes narrowed to slits. With lightning-fast action she double-pumped her new weapon, leveled it at Daniel's head, and through gritted teeth hissed, "Hasta la vista, baby!" Daniel never knew what hit him.

Over the years her brothers have learned never to underestimate their little sister. (I pray daily for her future husband!)

To Carrie's credit, she refused to allow her oppressors to rob her of her joy. She was having a party, and she was going to enjoy herself!

God has made abundant joy available to His children, but we typically experience far less than He wants us to.

GOD'S GIFT OF JOY

Stereotypes abound of what really spiritual people are like. Often we picture them as solemn sages who hoist the burdens of the world upon their shoulders. They give all their money to the poor and pray constantly, using King James English.

But there's another way to recognize a close walk with God—a Christian's level of joy.

When Jesus was born, the angel announcing His miraculous birth to the shepherds declared, "I bring you good tidings of *great joy*" (Luke 2:10). The story of Jesus is one of immeasurable joy. When Jesus taught His disciples what it would mean for them to have a close relationship with Him, He explained, "These things I have spoken to you, *that My joy may remain in you,* and *that your joy may be full*" (John 15:11). If you want to know if Christians are experiencing all God has provided for them in Christ, examine their joy. Joy in their lives reveals that they understand what God has done for them and what He's presently making available to them.

Jesus also promised His disciples that the joy He gave them was something "no one will take from you" (John 16:22). No one and nothing can steal your joy when Christ gives it to you.

> *If you want to know if Christians are experiencing all God has provided for them in Christ, examine their joy.*

A HIGH JOY THRESHOLD

One of the most beloved biblical accounts of joy is that of Paul and Silas in Philippi (Acts 16:11–25). These righteous men were on their way to pray when they encountered a demon-possessed slave girl. She was being exploited by men who sold her powers of divination. Paul eventually freed her from the demon, bringing her divining powers to an end. This infuriated her masters, who saw their ability to make a fortune from her slip through their fingers.

These frustrated entrepreneurs dragged Paul and Silas before the magistrates and made false accusations: "These men, being Jews, exceedingly trouble our city; and they teach customs which are not lawful for us, being Romans, to receive or observe" (verses 20–21). This was a lie. They just wanted vengeance.

The magistrates ordered soldiers to beat Paul and Silas with rods. Such an ordeal could break bones and was often lethal. The authorities laid "many stripes on them" (verse 23) and then threw them into the inner prison. The jailer, leaving nothing to chance, restrained their feet in stocks.

> *We would easily understand if at that point they bitterly questioned God's love for them.*

Paul and Silas, though innocent of any crime, had been publicly slandered and brutally beaten. They were consigned to a maximum-security prison like hardened criminals. They spent the long night on the cold, hard floor, their bruised and bleeding legs locked in stocks. Paul and Silas could easily have become angry at the cruel injustice meted out to them. Every bone in their bodies throbbed with pain. If there was ever a time someone could be excused for not being joyful, this was it.

At midnight Paul and Silas were still awake. Their excruciating situation did not lend itself to slumber. We would easily understand if at that point they bitterly questioned God's love for them or made plans to abort their missionary journey and head for home. But, incredibly, we read that they were *singing*—and not the blues, but hymns of praise to God.

How could they do that? What did they have to praise God for? How did they have the physical strength to sing after their harsh mistreatment? How could they have *joy* in such dismal circumstances?

Paul and Silas were experiencing this divine truth:

> **We determine the amount of joy we experience from God.**

This story teaches an important life lesson. Jesus promised that no one could take His joy away from believers (John 16:22); Paul and Silas proved this to be true. When these two men were unfairly abused, they had to make a choice. They could let resentment overtake their hearts, or they could allow Christ to fill them with His joy even in that awful situation. They chose joy.

The reality is, no one can steal our joy, but we can surrender it at any point we choose. When we face bleak situations as Paul and Silas did, we determine our own joy threshold. We decide the level of discomfort at which we will yield our joy to our circumstances.

Some people have an extraordinarily low threshold. A car cuts them off in traffic, and their joy is out the window. For others, any form of criticism or lack of appreciation drives their joy away. The potential joy stealers are numerous: job dissatisfaction, unexpected bills, a delayed flight, or a computer virus, for example. More serious events such as critical illness, death of a loved one, divorce, financial hardship, and abuse can all be devastating. But do these things have to drive joy from our lives?

In every difficult circumstance, *we* decide if that situation is significant enough to steal our joy.

What is your joy threshold? What does it take for you to lose your joy? Paul and Silas were adamant that not even an illegal, unfair beating and cruel imprisonment could rob them of the joy of knowing Christ. They had an exceedingly high joy threshold. How high is yours?

JOY-STEALING PHONE CALLS

During one span of a few months while Lisa and I were in seminary in Texas, our joy was challenged by an onslaught of onerous phone calls, plus other trials.

I was in my first semester of the PhD program and was feeling way out of my league. We had a one-year-old son and were expecting our second child. Lisa was working full time, and I carried a full load of doctoral seminars. One day we received a distressing call that Lisa's father had undergone triple-bypass heart surgery and had suffered a heart attack on the operating table. He was in critical condition. We dropped everything and flew to Canada to be with him. We waited for a week as Lisa's father slowly recovered, and then I returned home; Lisa stayed another week and then flew home, arriving late at night.

At four o'clock the next morning, just a few hours later, we received another phone call. Lisa's father had suffered a second heart attack and passed away. I took Lisa, who hadn't yet unpacked her suitcase, and headed back to the airport to fly to Canada for the funeral.

For these trips, Lisa had to take time off work without pay. We were penniless students and had no savings. We didn't know how we would pay our rent with Lisa missing three out of four weeks of work.

Later that same month another phone call came. This time we learned that Lisa's mother had been diagnosed with cancer and needed surgery immediately.

A month later the phone rang again. My sixteen-year-old sister, Carrie, had been diagnosed with an advanced case of Hodgkin's disease. She would have to undergo intensive and aggressive chemotherapy. Her cancer was extensive, and the odds were not good.

Meanwhile, our baby son suffered a seizure in his sleep, and we had to rush him to the hospital. More bills. Our second son was born under stress by C-section—even more bills.

During those traumatic months, our response to these difficulties was always our own decision. Despite the pressures of my postgraduate work, two babies, a critical lack of finances, and a steady stream of heart-wrenching phone calls, Lisa and I had to choose what we would allow to take away our joy. Would it be having more bills than money? Would it be the exhausting pressure of two little boys, one of whom hated to sleep at night? Would it be the serious illnesses of our family members? Would it be a funeral?

All these were difficult issues. Yet God had made His divine joy available to us. Even in the midst of the most painful experiences in our lives, we still knew that He loved us, that He was walking with us, and that in the end He would make all things right. The peace of God that surpasses all understanding (Philippians 4:7) stood guard over our hearts and allowed us, as a young family, to continue to have joy in our home.

> *Lisa and I had to choose what we would allow to take away our joy.*

KEEP GOING!

When our boys, Mike and Daniel, were young, Daniel was always trying to keep up with his older, faster brother. One day Lisa and I were sitting in the front yard when Mike raced past us. He approached a large puddle of water that had accumulated from a recent rainfall. Without breaking his stride, he gracefully leaped over the water like a gazelle and continued on his way. Moments later Daniel came chugging along. Realizing his beloved older brother had successfully overcome the obstacle, he sped up as fast as his short legs would carry him and made a heroic leap. He landed with a resounding splash in the middle of the puddle. Gathering himself back up and wiping muddy water from his face, he muttered, "These things never work out for me!" But he promptly continued to chase after his brother. Poor Daniel experienced his share of setbacks, but he never let them keep him down.

I work with a dynamic group of Christian CEOs. These men and women are in high-pressure jobs as they lead some of America's largest companies. As Christians, many of them have faced unfair criticism and even persecution for their faith and values. Some have been fired or bypassed for promotions. Others have been viciously criticized by the media for their stands on moral principles.

It has been rewarding to see these fine Christians cling to their joy in the face of painful opposition. God has helped them gain His perspective on their circumstances. The Holy Spirit residing within them has ministered to their hearts even when the world endeavored to discourage and destroy them. They've followed the words of the psalmist:

> *In high-pressure jobs leading some of America's largest companies, many Christian CEOs have faced unfair criticism and even persecution.*

"Many sorrows shall be to the wicked; but he who trusts in the LORD, mercy shall surround him. Be glad in the LORD and rejoice, you righteous; and shout for joy, all you upright in heart!" (Psalm 32:10–11).

Rejoicing in the Lord is a choice we make, one that goes deeper than our present feelings. As we consider all God has done for us and all He will do for us, we have every reason to be joyful.

OVERCOMING OUR BAD DAYS

Joy is one of the greatest evidences for the truth of Christianity. Let's face it, we all have bad days.

Take the young man walking down the street in Monterrey, Mexico. As he passed over a manhole cover, a methane gas explosion propelled the lid—and the young man—eight yards into the air. As the man soared upward, he struck a live, exposed electrical wire, giving him second-degree burns. As he descended, he landed on the roof of a passing bus, which screeched to a halt. The young man managed to give his rescuers his name before passing out. He'd suffered fractures to his arm and hip along with burns and bruises. As one television news reporter described the incident, "It was a case of someone being in the wrong place at the wrong time." Talk about a bad day.

Recently I had my own bad day. I was in Bakersfield, California, where I'd been speaking at a convention. I fly a lot and I'm a pretty careful traveler (I know what can go wrong), so I went to the airport two hours early. There I was informed my flight was an hour late, which meant I would have only fifteen minutes to make my connection in San Francisco for my flight home to Calgary. I decided not to fret but to use the time to get some work done. I took an escalator down to Gate 6 and settled in with my laptop for the wait. Finally the plane arrived.

The gate agent came on the loudspeaker announcing that the flight was now ready to board. I handed the agent my boarding pass and walked out on the tarmac to the plane. I had a seat on the exit row, and no one was sitting beside me. I would have lots of room!

I noticed the flight attendant walking down the aisle counting the passengers. Everything seemed fine.

As we began taxiing to the runway, the captain came on the loudspeaker. "Ladies and gentlemen, welcome aboard. We're expecting a smooth, quick trip over *to Los Angeles*..."

My heart jumped to my mouth. I was on the wrong plane! Instead of getting home that afternoon, now I wasn't sure what *day* I would arrive.

I started to beckon to the flight attendant to stop the plane and let me off—but then I'd have to endure the shame of everyone on board knowing what a fool I was. So I sat quietly during takeoff, trying desperately to figure out what to do.

When I landed in Los Angeles, I e-mailed my wife that I wouldn't be home for dinner and told her why. Then I had to face a customer-service agent and explain why my baggage was in San Francisco and I was in L.A. (I'm sure I detected a suppressed grin on her face.)

While I waited for the agent to search her computer for available flights, I checked my e-mail on my handheld. There was a message from my loving wife. I clicked open her e-mail, expecting words of sympathy and concern. Instead I found a whole line of HA-HA-HAs. She informed me that when she read what her travel-savvy, hundred-thousand-miles-per-year frequent-flyer husband had done, she laughed so hard her sides were hurting.

> *I sat quietly during takeoff, trying desperately to figure out what to do.*

I indignantly told the airline agent what my unsympathetic wife had just sent me, and she started laughing too. It turned out her husband had recently done the same thing.

Finding myself in that predicament, I had a decision to make. I could spend the rest of the day (or week, depending on available seats) frustrated and angry at myself or at the airline, or I could laugh at myself and allow the Lord to redeem the lost time.

Getting on the wrong airplane doesn't necessarily have to ruin your day. So even when my daughter called my cell phone to ask me to pick her up a Goofy hat at Disneyland (since I was in the area), and my son sent an e-mail asking for a Lakers jersey, I still had joy. On that day I asked God to raise my joy threshold to a level that could endure travel mishaps like that.

So what is your joy threshold? Can it sustain you on a bad day?

Spreading the Joy

Too many Christians underestimate the power of joy. Trying so hard to be "spiritual," we fail to realize that sometimes the most spiritual thing we can do is be joyful.

When I first became a seminary president, I greatly missed being a pastor. I had loved preaching each Sunday and shepherding my flock. Instead, I was going to the office each day and working my way through reams of paperwork.

One day my pastor called and asked if I would conduct a worship service for him that evening at a retirement home. It was my first chance to preach since leaving the pastorate, and I was itching to get back into the pulpit. I told myself, "These people don't know what they're in for tonight! After all, I've been a successful pastor, I have a PhD, and I'm a seminary president. I'm going to address in one sermon all the life questions senior adults generally ask. I may even do a Greek word study on the term *retirement*." I began digging into biblical commentaries and my Greek New Testament.

Later that afternoon I told my wife I would be going out after dinner to lead the service at the retirement home. Immediately she mentioned that she and the kids would like to come too; they missed having me as their pastor, and they thought it would be fun.

I quickly tried to douse that idea. "Lisa, it isn't going to be *fun;* I'm going to be doing *ministry!*"

Undeterred, Lisa insisted. She promised they wouldn't get in my way while I ministered to the seniors.

I had to warn her: "Now, Lisa, if you come, you must realize I'm going to stay there until I've spoken to every last person seeking my counsel. Many of these people are reaching the end of their life, and they may desperately need my advice. You and the children can't be tugging at my sleeve asking to go home."

She promised that the kids would bring books to read while they waited and would stay out of my way until my work was done. She assured me I wouldn't even know they were there.

So they came.

That night was one of the most unusual services I ever conducted. Throughout the entire worship experience, all I saw were the sides of peoples' faces. Everyone was looking to the left side of the room. At first I suspected this might be a home for people with neck conditions. Then I realized everyone in the room was staring at my three kids. Some ladies sitting in the row behind my children were reaching out and patting them on their heads. A lady farther back was blowing kisses at my daughter. Two old men were having a pretend gunfight with my boys. *No one* was listening to me.

> *There was an instantaneous stampede.*

I finally decided to bring my sermon to a premature close. I didn't even use my Greek word.

As I concluded the service I announced, "If any of you would like to meet my family, they're right..." There was an instantaneous stampede. Men and women crowded around my wife and kids. They were giving treats to my children and telling them jokes. Grandmothers were asking my wife about the kids' clothes. Not one person spoke to me.

Soon I was ready to go home. I made my way through the thick crowd to tell Lisa it was time to go. She informed me (rather smugly, I thought) that she and the kids couldn't leave until they'd talked with *every* person who wanted to speak with them, and I would have to wait. (I should have brought a book!)

As I stood waiting for the crowd to disperse, I saw something that made me gasp. An elderly, feeble-looking woman was slowly pushing a walker down a long hallway. The walker had a basket for her purse and other personal items. Inside that basket sat my eight-year-old son, Mike! I could envision this poor woman having a heart attack or suffering a hernia from pushing him down the hallway. "Mike!" I shouted. "Get out of that woman's basket!"

The woman slowly turned around, smiled, and said, "I *told* him to get in. I'm giving him a ride."

My poor son shrugged his shoulders as if to say, "Dad, what could I do? The lady told me to get into her basket!" He gave me a pitiful wave as he continued his way down the long hallway. He shouted, "Dad! Don't leave without me!"

When the lady finally made it to the end of the hall, I called out, "Mike, get out of there now, and be sure to say thank you for the ride."

The lady waved her hand dismissively and said, "Oh, that's okay. I'll bring him back!" With that she began to slowly inch him back down the hallway to where I was waiting. By the time they returned, most of the people had cleared out of the room. I yanked Mike out of the basket and said to the woman, "Well, I guess you'll need to be going back to your room to rest."

She looked at me with surprise and said matter-of-factly, "I still have to give a ride to the other two children!"

With that, my six-year-old son, Daniel, dutifully climbed into her basket and away they went.

By the time the woman returned with Carrie, it was past visiting hours, and the nurses were making announcements on the loudspeakers that visitors should already have left the premises.

As we finally got into our car and pulled out of the darkened parking lot, my son Mike broke the silence by asking, "Dad, why did those people do that?"

How do you answer a question like that? "Son," I replied, "tonight God saw that these people needed joy, and He knew you kids had a lot of joy to give. I hope that for the rest of your lives, whenever God knows of people who need joy, He can always count on you to give it." Those senior adults didn't need another sermon that evening. They wanted someone who could dispense joy. I also realized you can't give what you don't have. That evening I had theology, biblical exegesis, and platitudes galore—but my children had the joy.

I've been haunted by the memory of a woman I once met who'd been married to a minister for twenty years. She sadly confessed, "There is no joy in our home." It's easy for committed Christians to become so engaged in the work of ministry that they lose sight of what Jesus said is the natural by-product of the Christian life.

> "Tonight God saw that these people needed joy, and He knew you kids had a lot of joy to give."

Does it surprise you that when Paul listed the fruit of the Spirit (Galatians 5:22–23), the second quality, after love, is joy? Joy is a crucial part of the Christian life, and yet it can easily be lost. I've known many Christian homes that were characterized by integrity, orthodoxy, morality, or evangelism, but not joy. I'm afraid too many Christians surrender their joy too easily. They would never think of giving up their doctrine or their faith, but they relinquish their joy without a whimper.

JOY LOST

Perhaps giving up joy too easily was Martha's problem.

Martha dearly loved Jesus and no doubt was thrilled when He agreed to come for lunch at her house. She probably hummed to herself while she baked her special dessert and as she dusted and cleaned the house. As she went to the market to pick up a few last-minute groceries, she may have cheerfully told her friends that Jesus was coming to *her* house that day! Back home, perhaps she regularly glanced out her window to see if she could recognize His familiar silhouette approaching.

But when He arrived, bringing along His twelve hungry disciples, her heart may have sunk. Those guys could really wolf down the sandwiches! And as fast as Martha fin-

> *Finally Martha exploded.*

ished pouring their iced tea, they were already holding up glasses for a refill. Then the oven timer went off. The cake was going to burn! Then Thomas asked if she had decaf. It was all too much.

The worst thing was her sister Mary, parked in there with all the disciples, listening to Jesus. "Wouldn't it be nice if we could *all* be having a good time listening to Jesus?" Martha fumed to herself. "But *someone* has to do all the work!"

Finally Martha exploded. She stormed into the living room. In front of all His disciples, she accused Jesus: "Lord, do You not care that my sister has left me to serve alone? Therefore tell her to help me" (Luke 10:40).

Martha had lost her joy. She probably never even noticed when it left. At first she'd been thrilled that Jesus was coming to have fellowship with her. She'd promised herself she would enjoy Jesus's presence as soon as her tasks were accomplished. But there always seemed to be more work to do.

Mary, on the other hand, continually found joy in her relationship with Jesus. She always delighted in His presence, and the more time she spent with Him, the greater the joy she experienced. In His presence, nothing else mattered. She loved to sit at His feet and listen to Him talk about life and the kingdom of God.

Have you known believers who lost their joy? They were ecstatic when they first became Christians. They couldn't believe what had happened to them. They couldn't get enough church. They loved to read their Bible. But somewhere along the way, their Christian life became a series of duties and obligations. It became work, and the joy departed. Rather than experiencing deeper and deeper levels of joy in the Lord, they reached their limit.

Jesus said when His joy is in us, our joy will overflow (John 15:11). That's because our limited, human bodies can't contain all the joy Jesus wants to share with us. There's too much for us.

God's joy is limitless. The only limit to the level of God's joy we experience lies with us.

JOY IN OUR HOME

God doesn't want us to experience joy only when we're worshiping Him or reading our Bible. He wants us to know His joy in everything we do.

Our lives ought to be characterized by continual, irrepressible joy whether we're at work or at home.

Lisa and I decided that if our children were going to grow up to love God as much as we did, they would have to experience the joy of the Lord. We didn't want our kids to think that being a Christian meant their lives were destined for drudgery. The Christian life ought to be the greatest, most exciting and fulfilling life you can live. Too many Christian homes fail to cultivate their joy, so it's lost through neglect.

Being aware of this, we worked hard to make our home an oasis of joy. We tried to go lightly on the official house rules, focusing on the majors such as character and respect, but not fretting over the little things. We stocked fun games at our house so our kids wouldn't always want to go to a friend's home.

As I mentioned earlier, my wife loves to have fun, so she was always coming up with another spontaneous adventure. Our family room was once transformed into a fort. On Saint Patrick's Day, our entire meal, including the rice, was green. The kids made movies. In one of them their ninety-year-old great-grandfather played a pirate, until a sea monster (looking suspiciously like a vacuum hose) dragged him to a gruesome death. When we built a new home, we designed it for family interaction as well as for hosting social gatherings. Over the years we've hosted everything from a college murder-mystery dinner to a Hawaiian luau for New Year's. We've held massive street-hockey tournaments, transformed our living room into an enchanted forest, and hosted an *I Love Lucy* party for teenage girls. Our home holds a lot of memories!

> *We worked hard to make our home an oasis of joy.*

A few summers ago Lisa and I realized we had succeeded in our goal of making our home a place of joy. The kids were out of school, and each evening we would gather around the kitchen table to play card games. One evening we were finishing dinner when the phone rang. It was for Mike, who was seventeen at the time. Some of his friends had just returned from a summer trip; they were hosting a get-together at their place. Mike was definitely interested. Then he paused, put his hand over the phone, looked at us and asked, "What are you going to be doing?"

"Oh, maybe play some card games," we told him. "Nothing you haven't been doing all summer. Go ahead with your friends. You'll have fun."

As Mike prepared to leave, he looked at us quite seriously. "Don't have fun while I'm gone!" he said.

"Mike," I replied, "what do you want us to do? Put on sackcloth and hum Gregorian chants until you return? Don't worry, we won't do anything special."

Still, he urged us to wait until he came back before starting any games. I reminded him that he probably wouldn't be home before midnight, and since I had to get up at six the next morning, I wasn't going to wait up for him.

That evening the rest of us played some card games, then I went to bed. Suddenly I heard footsteps bounding up the stairs. My bedroom door burst open. "You didn't wait!" Mike bellowed accusingly, then added, "Stay right there!" He spun around and raced back down the stairs. Of course I wasn't going anywhere.

Minutes later, Mike reentered our bedroom along with the rest of the family. They had popcorn, cold drinks, and nachos. Everyone climbed on our bed, and Mike began dealing cards. "You don't even have to get out of bed," he explained.

It was around two in the morning before the kids finally left us to go to sleep.

For the remainder of that short night I was wiping corn chips and popcorn from my bed sheets. But we'd had fun. When it dawned on me that our seventeen-year-old party-animal son was hesitant to go out with his friends for fear he would miss out on the fun at home, I knew we'd achieved a home of joy.

The Challenge

Don't take joy for granted. The world has many ways of stealing it from you, but as with every aspect of our relationship with God, there are ultimately no limits to the joy we can experience. The potential for joy in our lives is boundless, and the only limits are what we impose on ourselves. If you allow yourself a low joy threshold, then every time you have a bad day or a difficult phone call, your joy will evaporate.

Ask the Lord to enlarge your joy capacity so it isn't vulnerable to every shift in the winds of life. Ask God to ground His work so firmly in your life that nothing robs you of the joy that comes from knowing you belong to God…and that He walks with you through every experience of life.

Questions for Reflection

1. How high is your joy threshold? How easily do you give up your joy?
2. What adjustments might you make so there's more joy in your life?

3. Are you like Mary or like Martha? Have you lost your joy in your
   relationship with Christ?

4. Take time to reflect on all God has made available to you, His
   child. Recall God's promises to you in the Bible. Allow God to
   minister to your heart and to rekindle His joy in your life.

SEVEN

OVERCOMING
OUR SPIRITUAL LIMITS

Have you ever been insulted by a warning label? Some instructions found on packages you purchase can be downright offensive to your intelligence.

A bottle of flavored milk carries this warning: "After opening, keep upright."

On a package of nuts: "Warning: Contains nuts."

For a set of shin pads: "Warning: Shin pads cannot protect any part of the body they do not cover."

On a camera: "This camera only works when there is film inside."

A bag of peanuts served by a commercial airline offers these helpful instructions: "Open packet, eat contents."

A package of pudding has this caution: "Warning: Product will be hot after heating."

A Swedish chainsaw manufacturer presents this sage advice: "Do not try to stop chain with hands." (Somewhere a handless Swede is in the midst of a nasty lawsuit.)

How about the iron that carries this profound wisdom: "Do not iron clothes on body." (We can only imagine.)

Finally, there's the warning on an electric router: "This product not intended for use as a dental drill."

Does it bother you that the kind of people who need these instructions are driving on the same roads you are?

While it seems incongruous for intelligent people to require such obvious guidance, the reality (and many a lawsuit) proves that plenty of people need such basic help.

But before we become too critical of those individuals, it might be good to review some rudimentary teachings God included in Scripture so you and I could avoid painful experiences.

INSTRUCTIONS FROM GOD

Think carefully about the invaluable guidance God is offering us in these passages:

"Well done, good and faithful servant; you were faithful over a few things, I will make you ruler over many things" (Matthew 25:21). As we discussed in an earlier chapter, if we're faithful in what God gives us, no matter how little, He *will* grant us greater responsibility in His kingdom. If God is not giving us more, we have evidently been careless managers of what we've already received.

"Then you will call upon Me and go and pray to Me, and I will listen to you. And you will seek Me and find Me, when you search for Me with all your heart" (Jeremiah 29:12–13). Do you feel alienated from God? Scripture promises that if we draw near to Him and fervently seek Him, He *will* draw near to us. If God seems far away, if you wonder if He's listening to your prayers, if your worship seems lifeless, then you may not have drawn near to Him as He desires.

"For assuredly, I say to you, if you have faith as a mustard seed, you will say to this mountain, 'Move from here to there,' and it will move; and noth-

ing will be impossible for you" (Matthew 17:20). Jesus assured us that if we have genuine faith, we'll pray for things that are impossible and they'll happen as we asked. If we aren't praying for God to do mighty things in our lives—and seeing God do those things—we aren't asking with the faith He requires.

"Come to Me, all you who labor and are heavy laden, and I will give you rest" (Matthew 11:28). Jesus is the source of spiritual rest. The refreshment He offers penetrates deeply into our souls. If our hearts and minds remain troubled, we've clearly not accepted Jesus's invitation to take our burdens to Him.

Scripture is filled with wisdom for living a successful, joyful life. Yet many of us are as reluctant to follow God's instructions as we are to read warning labels on merchandise. We ignore God's counsel at our peril.

Millions of people live their Christian lives far below the level God intends. Even though the Bible clearly tells us how to enjoy abundant life, we often ignore those admonitions and stumble along in spiritual failure and weakness. God has told us how to go to the next level with Him; we choose to disregard His Word.

REACHING THE LIMIT

Several years ago I had one of the early cell phone models. After a year I became extremely frustrated with it. The phone wasn't charging properly. I would leave it plugged in all night, yet the next day the battery was still low. I should mention that I don't have a mechanical bone in my body. I couldn't tell the difference between a carburetor and a colander. The cause of my problem may seem readily apparent to you, but the answer wasn't so obvious to me.

One day as I looked at the power charger plugged into the wall at one end and into my cell phone at the other, it hit me. My power cord must not be properly conducting electricity to my cell phone. I knew there was power in the wall, but the current was obviously not making it to my phone.

Without taking time to think further on the matter, I detached the cord from my cell phone, leaving the other end plugged into the wall. Then I licked the plug to determine if any electricity was coming through. Instantly I felt a painful shock course through my body. I saw a flash before my eyes. My tongue burned. My hair was standing on end.

As I staggered out of my office into the kitchen to my wife, I looked at her with a dazed expression and moaned, "You won't believe what I just did."

I've tried to find a way to put the best spin on what I did that day, but I have yet to find anyone who will agree that licking the plug was the logical thing to do.

There are ways to determine whether God's power is still flowing into your spiritual life. Ask yourself:

- When was the last time I became excited about something God showed me in His Word?
- Have I recently overcome a sinful habit or attitude?
- When did I last encounter Christ so powerfully that I didn't want the experience to end?
- When was the last time God used my life to bless someone in a manner God had never worked through me before?
- Is my trust and confidence in the Lord growing? What is the evidence?

- How's my prayer life? Am I spending more time in prayer than I did before, or less? What have I been hearing God say to me in prayer? What kind of answers am I receiving to my prayers?

Stalling out at your present level doesn't mean you have no spiritual life, but it does suggest your Christian growth has reached a plateau. You may still read your Bible daily, but it isn't impacting your life in new and deeper ways. You may still be walking with God, but perhaps you haven't learned anything new about Christ for some time. You may still be trying to serve the Lord, but you know He could be using your life more powerfully than He is.

> *What is the evidence that your trust and confidence in the Lord are growing?*

With our busy, overcommitted lives, Christians can feel overwhelmed at the thought of seeking to experience more of God. Growing closer to God doesn't have to involve climbing a mountain to commune with Him, spending prolonged times in intense fasting and prayer, or memorizing books of the Bible—although who wouldn't benefit from these efforts? Going deeper with God means moving from where we are to a new place with God. It involves attaining a higher level spiritually. It entails knowing Christ better than ever before.

NOT GOOD ENOUGH!

Lisa and I have been negotiating our way through parenting three teenage kids. We finally got two into their twenties, and we have one to go. For the most part they're a lot of fun, but they also know how to egg their dad on. They've learned that no phrase disturbs me more than this one: *It's good enough.*

It happens like this: "Son, I saw a lot of snow still sitting on the driveway and sidewalk. I thought you said you shoveled the driveway."

"Dad, it's good enough."

"I thought your history paper had to be twelve pages. This is only ten. Don't you need to work a little more on it before you submit it?"

"Dad, it's good enough!"

"I thought I asked you to make sure the kitchen was clean when Mom and I came home. There are still dishes everywhere."

"Dad, it's good enough…"

You get the idea. Of course, my kids know that at this point a rousing speech will well up within my breast and I'll begin to pontificate: "When you're a preacher, or a brain surgeon, or an accountant,

> *I'll probably never do anything the best, but I owe it to myself and others to do my best.*

do you think people will be satisfied with your sloppy work when you shrug your shoulders and say, 'It's good enough'? *It's never good enough unless it's your best!*"

Before I reach my climactic pronouncement, they'll have already begun rolling their eyes and edging toward the nearest exit.

I guess it's a quirk with me, but I have a profound awareness that I have only one life to live and it's passing by quickly. It's foolish to be cavalier with the few years of life we have. I'm not overly bright or talented, so I'll probably never do anything *the* best, but I owe it to myself and to those whose lives I touch to do *my* best. I don't want to reach the end of my life and be haunted by questions of what *might* have been. I want to know I lived my life to its ultimate potential and that God used me to extend His kingdom. God knows what He's capable of doing through my life. I want Him to do the maximum.

Refuse to Accept the Limits

Throughout history, certain people have been unwilling to accept limitations. For example, Edmund Hillary, a New Zealander, became fascinated by the various attempts of the world's great adventurers to scale the summit of Mount Everest.

In 1852 Mount Everest was identified as the tallest point on the planet at 29,028 feet. People naturally began vying to be the first person to reach the top of the world. Over the next century at least fifteen expeditions set out to reach the summit, resulting in at least two dozen deaths. With oxygen dangerously thin at that altitude, the treacherous crevasses and the shifting snow made scaling the mountain seem physically impossible.

Finally, on May 29, 1953, Edmund Hillary and Tenzing Norgay were the first people to reach the top. They instantly became international heroes. Hillary was eventually knighted for his heroic feat. What had appeared impossible had at last been accomplished. In the ensuing years, many more people would successfully reach the top, but only after Hillary and Norgay proved it could be done.[5]

Only a year after Everest was first scaled, another physical limit was overcome: the four-minute mile. Roger Bannister, a British medical student, was intrigued with breaking this record that had held the world's greatest athletes at bay. On May 6, 1954, at

> *What we require today are spiritual Hillarys and Bannisters.*

the Iffley Road Track in Oxford, Bannister challenged the hitherto unbreakable time barrier. Bannister broke the record, running the mile in three minutes, 59.4 seconds. Like Hillary, Bannister immediately became a hero and was eventually knighted.

Significantly, after the centuries it took for someone to achieve this incredible feat, Bannister's record was broken within two months: John Landry of Australia bested Bannister's time at three minutes, 57.9 seconds.[6] Others quickly followed. The sports world is accustomed to this phenomenon. Whenever someone sets a new record, athletes everywhere strive to best it. Most athletes spend enormous effort trying to beat their *own* personal best.

What we require today are spiritual Hillarys and Bannisters. We need people who refuse to accept the spiritual limits that have impeded other Christians. We need men and women who will pay the price required to go to a level with God that no one in their generation has yet achieved. People want to see what it looks like to overcome spiritual limits and to experience the joy of relating to God in a new dimension.

We encounter numerous spiritual limitations. We face the limit of not knowing God's way of thinking (Isaiah 55:8–9); though God tells us His thoughts, we often fail to grasp them. God's power is infinite (Isaiah 40), yet many Christians experience only a small amount of divine strength in their daily living. God's presence brings unmitigated joy (Psalm 16:11), yet there are thousands of joyless Christians. Jesus offers peace for our greatest trials (Matthew 11:28–29), yet many Christians remain heartbroken and anxious. Christians needlessly allow obstacles to prevent them from experiencing the full measure of what God has prepared for them.

In order to triumph over unnecessary spiritual hindrances, let's consider the following realities:

1. God wants us to overcome our spiritual limits. His promises to us are sincere. When He makes offers such as "Seek, and you will find" (Matthew 7:7), He means it! Any promise you find in Scripture reflects

God's desire for you. Don't dismiss a divine pledge because you don't believe it is possible. If God promised it, it *is* achievable.

2. God stands ready to give His people victory in every area of life. The psalmist David experienced God's presence firsthand and declared, "You are the God who does wonders; You have declared Your strength among the peoples. You have with Your arm redeemed Your people" (Psalm 77:14–15). David saw the Lord take impossible situations and produce complete victory. Likewise, God is prepared to overcome any obstacle that prevents us from going deeper with Him.

3. We must make every effort to incorporate God's promises into our lives. Paul urged the Christians in Philippi to "work out your own salvation with fear and trembling" (Philippians 2:12). Paul highlighted a great paradox of the Christian life. While God is the One who ultimately accomplishes His work in our lives, He doesn't override our complacency. God will not give us a dynamic, mature Christian faith if we're content with an immature, shallow one. Those men and women who reached the highest summits of Christian experience were willing to pay a higher price than their contemporaries to know God. God's promises are before us, but we must decide how much we want to experience them.

4. The rewards for striving for higher levels with God are incalculable. Each new degree of the Christian life has fewer and fewer people who attain it. Yet those who experience deeper intimacy with God eagerly testify to the wonder of knowing Him so deeply. How can you place a value on knowing and experiencing more of God? The reward is worth any effort or sacrifice. As the apostle Paul declared, everything else in life is worthless compared to knowing Christ (Philippians 3:8).

In light of all God wants to do in our lives, and knowing He has the power to set us free from our limitations, let's examine three factors that continue to hold us back from experiencing the full Christian life.

Sin Holds Us Back

Nothing stunts our spiritual growth more than sin. The writer of
Hebrews urged his readers, "Let us lay aside every weight, and the sin
which so easily ensnares us, and let us run with endurance the race that
is set before us" (12:1). If growing to know God more is like climbing
a mountain, then sin is excess baggage. It weighs us down, trips us up,
and wears us out. It keeps us from ascending to the spiritual heights we
could reach if we traveled unencumbered. The Bible says sin ultimately
leads to death (Romans 6:23).

In his book *Into Thin Air,* Jon Krakauer tells of a 1996 ascent of
Mount Everest when nine climbers perished. He recounts the story of
Sandy Pittman, a wealthy socialite who yearned to reach the top of Everest. Along with her climbing gear, she packed two laptops, a video camera, four cameras, two tape recorders, a CD player, a printer, eighty
pounds of satellite-telephone equipment, solar panels, batteries, gourmet
coffee, and an espresso maker.[7] Before she reached the mountain's summit, she would discard every nonessential piece of baggage. Finally she
had to be towed and carried to make it to the top.

Likewise, reaching new spiritual heights requires us to make adjustments along our journey. The writer of Hebrews exhorts us to disen-
tangle ourselves from every sin that's tripping us up. As long as we
stumble along in our sin, we'll fall short of God's best.

The great saints of church history were characterized by total surrender to God. They submitted every area of their lives to Him so they
were free to attain new spiritual heights.

V. Raymond Edman wrote a great book titled *They Found the
Secret: 20 Transformed Lives That Reveal a Touch of Eternity.* He
described twenty people who reached extraordinary spiritual heights,

including well-known Christians such as Hudson Taylor, Charles Finney, Dwight L. Moody, Amy Carmichael, and Oswald Chambers. Edman observed:

> The deep dealing of God with His children varies in detail but the general pattern seems much alike for individual cases. Into each life there is an awareness of failure, a falling short of all that one should be in the Lord; then there is a definite meeting with the risen Savior in utter surrender of heart, which is indeed death to self. There follows an appropriation by faith of His resurrection life through the abiding presence of the Holy Spirit. As a result there is realized an overflow of life.[8]

Edman concluded that only when these Christians grew dissatisfied with their spiritual condition and hungered for more were they prepared to do whatever was necessary to achieve greater spiritual heights. Each came to a point of personal surrender they'd never experienced. While they

Suppose you experience a restless spirit...

previously considered Christ to be their Lord, they had never wholly yielded themselves to God. They had attitudes, private sins, pride, and resentment that were draining them of the spiritual vitality they craved. When they consecrated themselves more thoroughly, they discovered God was waiting to meet them at an entirely new level. They began to experience a walk with Christ they never imagined was possible. Their lives and the fruit of their ministries thereafter testify to the enormous difference this new spiritual dimension made.

Take a moment to personalize this process. Suppose that you, too, experience a restless spirit. You feel a persistent discomfort that your relationship with God is falling short of what it could be. You read your Bible daily and stay active in your church. You've been a Christian for years, but you sense you should have stronger faith and a more fervent love for God. You know God could be using your life in greater ways than He presently is.

You decide to adopt the prayer of the psalmist: "Search me, O God, and know my heart; try me, and know my anxieties; and see if there is any wicked way in me, and lead me in the way everlasting" (Psalm 139:23–24).

As you invite the Spirit to scrutinize your life for anything that might be hindering your spiritual growth, He might bring to mind someone from whom you're estranged. Perhaps someone in your church let you down and betrayed your trust. To make matters worse, she never apologized or acknowledged the hurt her actions caused you. Now every time you see her in the church foyer, the two of you awkwardly pass in silence. You've been waiting for an apology, but meanwhile bitterness has festered in your heart.

When you ask the Lord what it will take for you to gain a more intimate, powerful walk with Him, the Holy Spirit makes a beeline for your broken relationship. The Spirit draws your attention to passages such as Matthew 5:23–24 and 5:38–44. Jesus made His views on forgiveness abundantly clear. The Spirit knows how debilitating unforgiveness is to your spiritual life.

As you stand convicted under the Holy Spirit's holy gaze, you acknowledge that your resentment is as wrong as God declares it to be. You ask God to forgive you, for you know that your unwillingness to forgive a friend is primarily a sin against God (Psalm 51:4). Then you pick up the phone to call your friend and mend your relationship. What matters now is not that your friend apologizes, but that you are set free from the anger and bitterness that has hardened your heart.

As you obey the Spirit, a profound freedom washes over your heart and mind. It surprises you, because you were unaware of how heavy this burden was that you carried by clinging to your anger. Now, that oppression is swept away and replaced by a sense of divine pleasure in your life. Your times of Bible study become fresh and exciting once again. Your heart grows tender toward God and His activity in other peoples' lives. Your joy returns (Psalm 51:12).

Like unforgiveness, every sin brings death to your spiritual life. It takes only one sin to bring your spiritual progress to a standstill. Imagine what several sins in your life, left unchecked, will do.

In particular, the sin of pride has an insidious way of burrowing its way into our souls. As Proverbs aptly warns, "Pride goes before destruction, and a haughty spirit before a fall" (16:18). Ironically, we can become so proud of our spiritual accomplishments that our boastfulness brings an end to them.

MISSIONARY PRIDE

In 1908, Canadian Presbyterian missionary Jonathan Goforth entered the city of Mukden to begin a series of revival meetings in Manchuria, China. Soon people were confessing grievous sins, and God's people were experiencing renewal.

One evening as Goforth sat on the platform during the time of hymn singing, he heard an inner voice whispering to him: *The success of these meetings is phenomenal. It will make you widely known, not only in China but throughout the world.*

Goforth had this reaction:

The human in me responded, and I experienced a momentary glow of satisfaction. Then immediately I saw that it was the evil one at work in his most insidious form, suggesting that I should divide the glory with the Lord Jesus Christ. Fighting the temptation down, I replied: "Satan, know once and for all that I am willing to become the most insignificant atom floating through space, so long as my Master may be glorified as He ought."[9]

The hymn ended and Goforth rose to speak. As he gave his message, the Holy Spirit convicted the audience of the truth of Goforth's words, and revival swept the congregation and the surrounding region. Fortunately, Goforth recognized that pride was threatening God's work and he quickly rejected it, freeing himself to serve God more powerfully in the coming days.

There are numerous sins which result in spiritual dullness. Greed, lust, anger, cynicism, envy, and selfish ambition can all eat away at your soul while you remain oblivious to their destructiveness. In each case, however, the Holy Spirit stands ready to cleanse and free you so you can draw closer to God.

Of course sin includes not only what we do wrong but also what we fail to do. Scripture warns, "To him who knows to do good and does not do it, to him it is sin" (James 4:17). You cannot enter God's presence and expect to enjoy a profound encounter with Him if you haven't done what you know He wants you to do.

> *There are numerous sins which result in spiritual dullness.*

That's the point of Matthew 5:23–24. Jesus explained that if we're at church in the act of worshiping God and we recall that someone is offended at us, we should leave the place of worship and hurry to be reconciled. Obedience to what we already know God has said is prerequisite to going any deeper in our walk with God.

FILED BUT NOT FOLLOWED

When I first became a seminary president, I felt overwhelmed by all I had to do. I'm a task-oriented person, and nothing piles up on my desk. My kids complain that if they set a glass of water on the kitchen counter for a millisecond, I'll immediately snatch it up and put it in the dishwasher. With this type of neurotic personality, I never felt my office work was done. During those days, before traveling out of town, I would catch up on my paperwork as much as possible so I wouldn't be too far behind when I returned. Then as soon as I arrived home, I would rush to my office to address any new work that had come in while I was away.

I occasionally felt convicted about neglecting my family through this constant work, but I always excused it with the explanation that I had so much to do. After all, this was the *Lord's* work!

One day I was preparing to travel to a conference in Texas. I decided to quickly run by the office that morning, then have coffee with my wife before heading to the airport. As soon as the staff noticed me walking down the halls, I was inundated with people needing to talk with me, just for a minute. My coffee date with my wife was reduced to a quick hug before I grabbed my suitcase and dashed out the door. As I drove to the airport, it dawned on me I hadn't even said good-bye to my kids.

Later, as I sat in the conference auditorium listening to sermons, the Holy Spirit spoke to me about practical ways I could minister to my family even while I held a demanding job. I pulled out a sheet of paper and hurriedly jotted down the many useful ideas He was giving me. The preacher must have thought his sermon was exceptional because I was taking notes as fast as I could write. The Holy Spirit gave me a full page of ideas on how I could be a better husband and father. I was eager to get home so I could implement these great plans. I stuffed the list into my Bible.

A colleague picked me up at the airport and dropped me off at home. One of the professors happened to be driving by my house as I arrived, and he pulled into my driveway to quickly let me know about something going on at the seminary. When I entered my house, I discovered that another thoughtful colleague had stopped by to drop off mail for me so I wouldn't have to go by the office. He was still at my house when I arrived, and he began to review with me the materials he was leaving. Then the phone rang—someone from the office.

I was immediately engulfed in my old routines.

For the next several months my life went on as it always had, but I was experiencing discontent as I struggled with a life that continued to be out of balance.

I stuffed the list into my Bible.

Meanwhile, I'd acquired a new Bible just after that Texas trip. One day I wanted to look something up in my old Bible. As I took the Bible from the top shelf in my office where I'd placed it, a sheet of paper fell out of it and fluttered to the floor. Curious, I picked up the paper. Instantly I began to tremble. There in my hands was the list of actions that I knew without question almighty God had given me. I had forgotten. I carefully read each item and remembered how powerfully God had spoken to me during that service. It became painfully clear to me why I hadn't been experiencing God's anointing on my life since that time. I had filed God's instructions instead of following them.

I moved that list to my new Bible. Every morning I would pull it out and ask the Lord to show me how to put each instruction into practice. Being a task-oriented person, I longed to transfer that list into my Completed file. But whenever I started to do so, the Lord gently instructed me to place it back in my Bible.

I'll never forget the satisfaction I felt on the day the Lord finally gave me the peace to put the list away because I was now regularly practicing what He had told me to do. Of course, the Lord soon introduced me to a whole new list.

If we won't be serious about dealing with our sin, we cannot expect to grow in our faith. If you want to move to a new level with God, take an inventory of what God has told you about your sin and consider what you've been doing about it.

LACK OF FAITH HOLDS US BACK

A second reason we don't grow spiritually is that we lack faith. God's power toward us is inexhaustible, but our trust in Him is limited. While God can do anything He chooses, the Bible says He responds to us according to our faith (Matthew 13:58).

In his classic book *Limiting God,* John Hunter provides a powerful analysis of Psalm 78, which looks at the Israelites' failure to enter the Promised Land. Hunter notes about verse 41:

> Verse 41 seems to gather together the whole idea and to sum up
> the effect of Israel's failure: "Yes, again and again they tempted

God, and limited the Holy One of Israel." What an unusual thought this is—that these people *limited* God. The Almighty Creator God was limited by the creature. They, of their own free will, shut themselves up in a wilderness. They pushed God into a corner. It wasn't that God was not strong enough or powerful enough, but that His people deliberately chose to limit Him!

They limited God in two distinct ways. First, they limited what God would do *for* them, and then they limited what God would do *through* them....

How amazing! Forty years later they still had not reached the land of Canaan! What could have been accomplished in days was finally completed in over forty years.... What could and should have been continuous forward movement—pressing on, counting on God's promise, expecting nothing but blessing—became a dismal failure. Their speed slowed down, and eventually they stopped. They ceased progressing and started to wander. They lost their vision of the Promised Land and were content with a much lower standard. Dissatisfaction, disappointment, disaster, and disobedience became the accepted norm of their daily lives. God was limited.[10]

Why does God do mighty works through some people and not others? It's a matter of faith.

Hebrews 11 provides a list of what God did through people who believed Him: Enoch "did not see death" (verse 5); Noah built a massive ark (verse 7); Abraham moved to a distant land (verse 8), then later prepared to sacrifice his only son (verse 17); Jacob blessed succeeding generations (verse 21); Joseph foretold events four hundred years in the future (verse 22); Moses rejected a prince's station to become a leader of slaves (verses 24–25), then led his people through the Red Sea (verse 29); Rahab was the lone survivor of her entire city (verse 31).

This chapter tells us also of people of faith who subdued kingdoms, performed righteous deeds, obtained divine promises, closed lions' mouths, quenched fires, escaped the sword, renewed their strength, fought heroically, routed enemy armies, and saw the dead arise (verses 33–35). Pretty impressive stuff!

And all this was accomplished because they trusted God. They did not limit what they believed God could do.

Jonathan Goforth, who witnessed God's amazing power firsthand, observed:

> Our reading of the word of God makes it inconceivable to us
> that the Holy Spirit should be willing, even for a day, to delay
> His work. We may be sure that, where there is a lack of fullness
> of God, it is ever due to man's lack of faith and obedience. If
> God the Holy Spirit is not glorifying Jesus Christ in the world
> today, as at Pentecost, it is we who are to blame. After all, what is
> revival but simply the Spirit of God fully controlling in the sur-
> rendered life? It must always be possible, then, when man yields.
> The sin of unyieldedness, alone, can keep us from revival.[11]

RÉSUMÉS AND A LACK OF FAITH

A frustrated pastor once asked me if I would distribute his résumé to churches needing a pastor. When I asked him why, he said the people in his church didn't want to go with God. He didn't want to waste his ministry on stubborn congregants.

I asked how long he'd been the pastor of his church.

"Two years," he responded.

> *"Do you get the impression that as your pastor I believe God can do anything?"*

"How long were you at your previous church?" I probed.

"A year and a half. But they didn't want to go with God either."

I suggested that he try something. I instructed him to approach the couple in his church who were the most supportive of his pastoral ministry and ask them, "When you hear me preach and teach and when you watch the way I lead the church, do you get the impression that as your pastor I believe God can do anything?" He agreed to do this.

Later he confessed that though this couple loved him dearly, they admitted he did not exude faith in the Lord, and so the church members lacked confidence too.

It had been obvious to me that this disgruntled minister did not believe God could do anything; if he had, he wouldn't have been trying to leave his church after only two years.

The evidence was there again: *we* limit God.

FAITH AND LEADING A CHURCH

I was privileged that my dad, who was simultaneously my pastor, really believed God could do anything.

I remember when he told our family that God was leading him to accept a pastorate in Saskatoon, Saskatchewan, Canada. In all my nine years growing up in Southern California, I'd never *heard* of Saskatoon. My dad excitedly described the vast regions across Canada that had no evangelical witness. He believed revival was coming to Canada, and he sensed God wanted to involve the church in Saskatoon. It all sounded pretty exciting to us.

Then we moved to Canada and saw the church. It was a dump— a tiny, ugly, old building in desperate need of repair, and there was no money for even a fresh coat of paint. The church had only ten members left, and some of them

> *I was raised in this atmosphere where people* expected *God to do the miraculous.*

didn't get along with one another. For the life of me I couldn't see what Dad was so excited about.

I learned that when Dad looked at something, he always saw it through eyes of faith. He viewed everything from the perspective of what God was capable of doing. He looked at a drab little run-down church building with hardly any members, and he saw God using it to start a thousand mission churches all over Canada.

Not surprisingly, Dad began to see his faith in God materialize. Even though our church had never sponsored a mission in its history, we began starting new missions every year. We established a Bible college to train people to serve in those new churches. Our college ministry flourished, and many of those we reached were called into full-time Christian service. People all over North America felt led to support the exciting work God was doing and donated hundreds of thousands of dollars to our little church. People drove more than a thousand miles just to attend a service at our church and to witness firsthand God's powerful activity in our midst.

I was raised in this atmosphere where people *expected* God to do the miraculous. God walked with my father and our church so practically and powerfully that my father later wrote what he learned in his book

Experiencing God: Knowing and Doing His Will, which has been read by millions of people around the world.

Sadly, after my father left Saskatoon to take on a new assignment, those who came behind him didn't see things through the same eyes of faith. Whereas the congregation used to routinely trust the Lord for funds, the Faith column soon disappeared from the budget. Unless the money was already in the bank, the church wouldn't move forward. Not surprisingly, donations stopped flowing in. Miracles quit happening. Excitement ebbed. The church that had repeatedly witnessed God's miraculous intervention began struggling to pay its bills. The congregation dwindled from a vibrant, growing church that believed God could do anything to a small remnant, once again grimly holding on to survive.

What happened to that congregation? Did God suddenly choose to love and care for it only when my family pulled into town? And then did God arbitrarily decide to stop the flow of His blessings after a new pastor came?

No. God's love for the church was always the same—before we came, while we were there, and after we left.

The same is true of His power. God has remained infinitely powerful throughout history. God never changes (Malachi 3:6). Since God is constant, the difference always lies with His people and whether we truly believe He is all-powerful.

While reading this book, you may have concluded that your faith needs to increase. Perhaps you're like that father who cried out in desperation over his demon-possessed boy, "Lord, I believe; help my unbelief!" (Mark 9:24). You believe God is powerful, but you want your faith to increase. There are things you long to see happen in your life that will occur only if you trust God for them. That father had enough faith for some things, but his son was still in bondage. The man wisely cried out to the Lord in spite of his doubts, and the Lord responded with a miracle.

As I said earlier, I'm a list person. So here's a suggestion. Make a list of particular situations and people for whom you're presently concerned.

Then add a second column and list what you sense God wants to do in each situation. For example, God may be leading you to go on a mission trip with your church. The trip costs two thousand dollars, and you need God to provide the fifteen hundred dollars you lack. Or you may long to talk with a family member about your faith in Christ, but you fear it will result in anger and rejection.

Now add a third column. In this one, for each need, write down whether you believe God is capable of meeting it. Don't simply give the expected Sunday school answer. Examine your heart. Consider how you're living. Do you *really* believe?

Spend time evaluating and praying over each item on your list. Allow the Holy Spirit to reveal areas where you must increase your faith. Be open and ready to obey what God tells you to do next. That's how you'll know if you truly trust Him. Only God can increase your faith, but you have to desire such an increase, just as that desperate father did.

Continue praying for those difficult situations, and ask God to help you trust Him for all He wants to do. Then watch expectantly for Him to act. Keep in mind that someone else's well-being may depend on your faith as you intercede for that person—as was true with the father and his demon-possessed son. Too much is at stake for you to remain content with your current level of faith.

LACK OF LOVE HOLDS US BACK

Most of the difficulties in the Christian life can be traced to a love problem. The apostle Paul claimed, "For the love of Christ compels us" (2 Corinthians 5:14). Paul realized that a Christian's greatest motivation is love for Christ. Such love inspires people to make any sacrifice, pay any price, and exert any effort Christ requires.

Jesus said, "He who does not love Me does not keep My words" (John 14:24). He also stated, "You are My friends if you do whatever I command you" (John 15:14). Our relationship with God is based on love; it's our love for Him that motivates us to continually pursue a deeper walk with Him.

Just as love between a husband and wife drives them to an increasingly intimate relationship, so our love for God compels us to move ahead in our walk with Him.

First Corinthians 13 is perhaps Scripture's greatest discussion of love. The apostle Paul concludes this passage with these words:

> When I was a child, I spoke as a child, I understood as a child,
> I thought as a child; but when I became a man, I put away
> childish things. For now we see in a mirror, dimly, but then face
> to face. Now I know in part, but then I shall know just as I also
> am known. (verses 11–12)

Paul connected godly love with spiritual maturity. I believe Paul was saying that love is never satisfied to remain in an immature relationship. Our love for God will stimulate us to continually seek to know Him at a deeper level.

TAKING OUR LOVE TO A HIGHER LEVEL

What if you realize your love for Christ has waned?

Through the righteous prophet Hosea, God demonstrated how He responds to His people when their hearts depart from Him. God told Hosea to marry Gomer, a woman of questionable character. Hosea loved her, cared for her, and provided for all her needs. Nevertheless, Gomer's heart was enticed by other men, and she eventually betrayed and abandoned her faithful husband. When God's people lose their love for Him, He views their betrayal as spiritual adultery (Hosea 3:1).

Hosea would have been justified in abandoning his philandering wife to her well-deserved fate, but he didn't.

> *Take note of those things that are more important to you than God.*

God told Hosea to pay any price necessary to win her back. Then Hosea took Gomer and isolated her from every temptation that had brought about her downfall. He spent long periods of intimate time with her and restored their love relationship (verses 3–4).

God declared He would act the same way toward those who forsake His love. He'll separate them from those things which have taken priority over Him. He'll spend time with them and renew their love for Him.

So what should you do if your heart has shifted from its love commitment to God?

First, take note of those things that have become more important to you than God.

Second, offer those things to God so they no longer control you. If your job consumes all your time and energy, God may lead you to change your employment. Or He may allow you to lose your job so you can find a position that doesn't make such exclusive claims on your life.

Third, spend prolonged time with God. This is a must if your relationship with Him is to be restored. Through the Scriptures and through meditation, God will remind you of His great love for you. Read the accounts of Christ's sacrifice on the cross for you. Recount your numerous blessings.

God wants your love. He is pursuing you just as Hosea sought Gomer. As you surrender to His love, He'll take you to an entirely new level in your walk with Him.

THE SECOND MILE

If you truly want to reach a new spiritual plane with God, you can be assured of this: God wants this for you too, and He'll see that you get there. He'll draw you into a deeper walk with Him.

My wife, Lisa, had one of those powerful going-to-the-next-level experiences. My brother Mel is the pastor of our church. He was preaching through a powerful series of sermons titled "Going the Second Mile" which he later published as a book.[12] Mel spoke about Jesus's command to His disciples to go further than was expected of them, especially in relating to enemies (Matthew 5:38–42).

During one particularly poignant message from Mel, Lisa felt deeply moved by the Holy Spirit to apply the lesson to her life. At the close of the service, she bowed and prayed: "Lord, I'm willing to go the second mile, but I don't know where that is. I have a good life, a wonderful husband [Hey, that's what she said!], three fantastic kids, a beautiful home, and a great church. My life is so good I don't know where my second mile even is. But if you'll show me where it is, I'll go there."

It didn't take long for Lisa to discover where her second mile was.

Less than two weeks later, she and our daughter Carrie decided to drive from our town into Calgary, about fourteen miles away. We'd experienced our first snowfall of the winter that morning. Later that day the sun came out and melted most of the snow from the roads, so Lisa decided to make a quick trip to a bookstore in the city.

They were on their way back, about five miles from home, when disaster hit. As they drove down the undivided highway, an oncoming vehicle was preparing to make a left turn. The driver came to a stop in the highway, waiting for Lisa to pass by. A second vehicle, a minivan, was following closely behind the turning car, and the driver was distracted. When she suddenly realized she was about to rear-end the vehicle in front of her, the driver frantically slammed on the brakes. She hit the only patch of ice left on that stretch of road, and her car was hurled into a wild 360-degree spin.

Carrie screamed just as Lisa noticed the van hurtling toward them. Both vehicles were traveling sixty miles an hour. Lisa swerved toward the shoulder, but it was too late. They collided head-on.

The crash was deafening. Airbags exploded open. The two minivans crumpled upon impact. Windows shattered.

Lisa's right kneecap was broken, and both she and Carrie were covered in cuts and bruises. The other driver suffered major injuries and was knocked unconscious. Incredibly, no one was killed.

I was in a lunch meeting when my phone rang. I noticed that the call was from Lisa's cell phone. Instead of Lisa, however, it was a stranger who told me in a shaken voice that my wife and daughter had just been in a head-on collision and would be taken by ambulance to a hospital.

When I arrived at the accident site, the highway was closed and vehicles were backed up in long lines in both directions. Emergency workers were using the Jaws of Life to free the trapped woman from her mangled vehicle. A helicopter was landing on the highway, waiting to airlift her to a hospital.

When I spotted the wreckage of our van sitting backward in the ditch, my stomach lurched. A small group of people huddled in the snow near our van. A stranger was holding my dazed daughter, who was covered in blood. My wife was lying in the ditch with an oxygen mask on her face and her leg contorted in an unnatural position. They were giving her morphine to relieve her agony.

Thus began one of the most difficult years of our lives.

For the next several days, Lisa endured unbearable pain. It would take multiple surgeries to put her knee back together. She spent months on crutches. In the middle of the night, her leg would undergo severe spasms, shaking the bed so violently it would wake us both. She suffered recurring nightmares of the accident and would wake up screaming. She began physiotherapy treatments three times a week, and the treatments were excruciating. She used to jog regularly and had recently competed in a 10k race; now she had to accept the fact she would probably never run again. Just walking up and down stairs was painful.

> *Thus began one of the most difficult years of our lives.*

Throughout this ordeal, many of our Christian friends offered advice. Their prevailing counsel was that we should file a lawsuit because we could make a lot of money.

I have to confess there were days when a lawsuit didn't seem like a bad idea—when I came home from work to find my poor wife lying in bed in agony, and I realized the only reason she was in this condition was someone else's carelessness.

One day Lisa told me she'd discovered the other driver's name. Lisa had written her a letter and wanted me to find her address.

I was curious to read that letter. It said this:

I am the woman who was driving the vehicle that was in the collision with you. I wanted you to know I was so glad to hear that you are going to be okay. I am a Christian, and I have been praying for you every day. Anyone who saw our vehicles claims it was a miracle we survived. I believe God must have a purpose for saving our lives. If you ever want to get together to talk about it, please give me a call.

Lisa had enclosed as a gift a little china plate that said, "Thank You, God, for our miracle."

I looked at Lisa in amazement. "This woman's carelessness almost killed you. You might walk with a limp the rest of your life—and you're sending her a gift?"

Then Lisa explained about the second mile. Two weeks earlier she'd asked God to show her where that was. "It didn't take God long to show me!" she exclaimed.

The next day when I arrived home, I made my trek up the stairs to see how Lisa was doing. She was excited. She had just hung up the phone after talking with Kathy, a wonderful Christian woman who's exceptionally evangelistic with all her neighbors. When Kathy learned the name of the other driver, she excitedly informed Lisa that the woman was her neighbor before Kathy

> *God gave her an opportunity to trust Him and serve Him at an entirely new level.*

had moved to a different home. When they still were neighbors, Kathy had invited this woman to church. She had shared the gospel with her on many occasions, but the woman hadn't responded positively. Even though many of Kathy's neighbors accepted Christ, this woman had not.

Hearing about the woman's involvement in the accident, Kathy immediately thought, *This may be what gets her attention and finally brings her to God.* Kathy gave Lisa the woman's address so Lisa could send her the letter and the gift. And over the phone, Lisa and Kathy prayed together for this woman.

I don't believe God caused Lisa to have that accident, but He did give her an opportunity to trust Him and to serve Him at an entirely new level. Lisa discovered that her "second mile" involved pain and suffering—but it also brought the thrill of knowing she was part of God's eternal plan. She experienced the joy of participating in His eternal purpose to reach out to someone He loves, and she was overjoyed to know God is definitely working in this woman's life. (As of this writing, she hasn't yet become a Christian. We'd appreciate your prayers.)

THE CHALLENGE

Today there are more Christians than ever before. There are also more churches and Christian organizations and ministries than at any time in history. Yet morally, spiritually, and socially, our world is getting worse.

Today there are a record number of unchurched people in North America. Western Europe is a spiritual wasteland. World religions that violently reject the claims of Christ control the lives of millions of people around the world.

What does all this mean? Despite millions of Christians today, our world is falling further and further away from God.

Something has to change. *We* must change. Clearly our current walk with God is inadequate. Obviously the ministry of many of today's churches is insufficient for the task of bringing our world to Christ. We must be willing to go to a deeper level in our relationship with Christ if He is to use us more powerfully. Our churches must become dissatisfied with their current level of divine service and cry out to God for a fresh awakening.

Are you ready for God to take you to a new level in your walk with Him? Do you hunger to know more of God? Do you want Him to use your life more powerfully to impact others?

God wants that too. He's prepared to take you to that place. But a deep walk with God does not come effortlessly. If it did, many more people would have one.

First, you must decide you're unwilling to remain where you are.

Second, you must be prepared to pay a price. Will you rise earlier so you can spend unhurried time with Him? Will you forgo comforts and pleasures so you can focus on your walk with Him?

God isn't looking for our lip service, as we tell Him how much we wish we knew Him better. He seeks a radical commitment to do whatever it takes to know Him the way we say we want to.

Are you willing to pursue God with all your heart? If you are, be prepared for an unbelievable adventure. You cannot begin to imagine all God has in store for you. You cannot fathom the infinite reward that awaits you for having pressed on to experience God in all His fullness.

Why don't you begin that journey today?

QUESTIONS FOR REFLECTION

1. Is the Holy Spirit making you restless about your walk with God? If so, how are you responding?

2. Take an inventory of your life. Are sins robbing you of the intimacy God desires to have with you? What has God told you to do that you aren't doing?

3. Evaluate your faith. Is there any issue in your life in which you're having difficulty trusting God? How does your life presently reflect your total trust in God for every situation and relationship?

4. Reflect on your love for God. Has your love for Him grown deeper over the years? Has anything in your life taken priority over God? What steps does the Holy Spirit want you to take so your love for God is rekindled?

5. Write down specific steps the Holy Spirit is leading you to take so you can move forward in your walk with God.

6. Consecrate this matter in prayer. Ask God to help you as you obey Him and press on to a new level with Him.

ACKNOWLEDGMENTS

I want to express my loving appreciation to my wonderful wife, Lisa, who was blissfully unaware that I slipped "perpetual editing" into our marriage vows!

Additional kudos to my good friends Bob Shelton, Hermann Brandt, Bo Stevens, and Ross and Phyllis Lincer, all of whom desire to go to a higher level with God. Each one offered helpful and unique insights into this book. Thank you!

Notes

1. Jonathan Goforth, *By My Spirit* (Grand Rapids, MI: Zondervan, 1942), 19.

2. Basil Miller, *Praying Hyde: A Man of Prayer* (Greenville, NC: Ambassador, 2000), 97–108.

3. Miller, *Praying Hyde*, 58–59.

4. Miller, *Praying Hyde*, 58–59.

5. Jon Krakauer, *Into Thin Air: A Personal Account of the Mt. Everest Disaster* (New York: Anchor Books, 1998), 13–15.

6. BBC On This Day, May 6, http://news.bbc.co.uk/onthis day/hi/dates/stories/may/6/newsid_2511000/2511575.stm.

7. Krakauer, *Into Thin Air*, 154.

8. V. Raymond Edman, *They Found the Secret: 20 Transformed Lives That Reveal a Touch of Eternity* (1960; repr., Grand Rapids, MI: Zondervan, 1984), 17.

9. Goforth, *By My Spirit*, 28.

10. John E. Hunter, *Limiting God: Updated Edition* (1966; repr., Kingsport, TN: Fresh Springs, 1995), 5–6.

11. Goforth, *By My Spirit*, 181.

12. Mel Blackaby, *Going the Second Mile* (Sisters, OR: Multnomah, 2006).

ABOUT THE AUTHOR

D r. Richard Blackaby is the president of Blackaby Ministries International (www.blackaby.org), where he works with his father, Henry, and speaks internationally on leadership and the Christian life. He has been a senior pastor and was a seminary president for thirteen years. He holds a bachelor's degree in history, a master's of divinity, a PhD in church history, and an honorary doctorate of divinity.

Richard is married to Lisa, and they have three children: Mike, Daniel, and Carrie. They live in Cochrane, Alberta, Canada.

Richard has also written *Putting a Face on Grace: Living a Life Worth Passing On.*

He also coauthored numerous books with his father, including these:

Experiencing God: Knowing and Doing His Will, Revised Edition

Blackaby Study Bible: Personal Encounters with God Through His Word

Hearing God's Voice

Called to Be God's Leader: How God Prepares His Servants for Spiritual Leadership

Spiritual Leadership: Moving People on to God's Agenda

Spiritual Leadership: The Interactive Study

Cross Seekers: Discipleship Covenant for a New Generation

Discovering God's Daily Agenda

The Experience: A Devotional and Journal

When God Speaks: How to Recognize God's Voice and Respond in Obedience

Experiencing God: Collegiate Edition